THE NOBLE REVERED

MUḤAMMAD

BETWEEN THE KHĀRIJIITE TERRORIST SAVAGES AND THE EXISTENTIALIST NIHILIST HATERS

Pencils And Cartoons Do Not Harm The Prophet Of Islām (صَلَّى ٱللَّهُ عَلَيْهِ وَسَلَّمَ): The Very One Who Judged The Khārijite Terrorists With Leaving The Fold Of Islām◈

Abu Iyaaḍ
Amjad bin Muḥammad Rafīq

Visit:
www.prophetmuhammad.name
to learn more about Islām and the Prophet.

◈ Numerous highly-regarded scholarly authorities, past and present, deduce from the Prophetic traditions that the Khārijites are outside the fold of Islām.

Title: The Noble, Revered Prophet of Islām, Muḥammad
Author: Abū Iyaaḍ Amjad bin Muḥammad Rafīq
Version: 5.00

1st print edition: Rabīʿ al-Awwal 1436H / January 2015CE.
Cover by A. Salaam Walker, Usul Design.

ISBN-10: 194284431X
ISBN-13: 9781942844310

Jointly published by:

Hikmah Publications
P.O. Box 44121
Philadelphia
PA 19144
United States

Salafī Publications
472 Coventry Road
Small Heath
Birmingham
B10 0UG
United Kingdom

Website: www.prophetmuhammad.name

Contents

Transliteration Table

Consonants

ء	ʾ	د	d	ض	ḍ	ك	k
ب	b	ذ	dh	ط	ṭ	ل	l
ت	t	ر	r	ظ	ẓ	م	m
ث	th	ز	z	ع	ʿ	ن	n
ج	j	س	s	غ	gh	ه	h
ح	ḥ	ش	sh	ف	f	و	w
خ	kh	ص	ṣ	ق	q	ي	y

Vowels

Short	ـَ	a	ـِ	i	ـُ	u
Long	ـَا	ā	ـِي	ī	ـُو	ū

Dipthongs	ـَوْ	aw	ـَيْ	ay

عَزَّ وَجَلَّ	The Mighty and Majestic.
سُبْحَانَهُ وَتَعَالَى	The Sublime and Exalted.
صَلَّى ٱللَّٰهُ عَلَيْهِ وَسَلَّمَ	May Allāh make good mention of His Prophet in the highest company and grant him safety.
رَضِيَ ٱللَّٰهُ عَنْهُ	May Allāh be pleased with him.
رَحِمَهُ ٱللَّٰهُ	May Allāh show mercy to him.
عَلَيْهِ ٱلسَّلَامُ	Peace be upon him.

Introduction

All praise is due to Allāh,[1] the Creator and Lord of the Worlds, the Lord of Noah, Abraham, Moses, Jesus and Muḥammad. May the peace and blessings be upon them all.

Tamīm al-Darī (رَضِيَ ٱللَّٰهُ عَنْهُ) - a Christian convert to Islām - narrated that the Prophet Muḥammad (صَلَّى ٱللَّٰهُ عَلَيْهِ وَسَلَّمَ) said, "*This affair (of Islām) will reach what the night and day reach (of all places on Earth) and Allāh will not leave a city-house or a desert-dwelling except that Allāh will enter this religion into (that household).*"[2] This promise was part-fulfilled in the early part of Islām in which acceptance of the Prophet's call spread through the entire Arabian peninsula and beyond. Statistics repeatedly demonstrate that Islām is the fastest growing way of life in the West. This phenomenon is not taking place because terrorists and fanatics are entering every household and forcing its inhabitants to convert or die. Rather, people in every household are hearing about Islām and the Prophet Muḥammad (صَلَّى ٱللَّٰهُ عَلَيْهِ وَسَلَّمَ) due to a combination of strongly negative media coverage and ease of access to information about Islām. The inquisitive, sincere person who looks beyond the propaganda, makes an objective, unbiased study and sees the beauty of Islām and the magnificent, unrivalled character of the Prophet (صَلَّى ٱللَّٰهُ عَلَيْهِ وَسَلَّمَ) will be led to accept Islām. A perfect illustration of this is in the Dutch politician, Arnoud Van Doorn.[3] In fact, this is how it used to be at the dawn of

[1] The name of this creator is Allāh (*īl, el, ilāh, iloh, elah*) in the languages of Hebrew, Aramaic (Syriac) and Arabic. This is not "*the God of the Muslims*" but the God of all Prophets, Messengers and mankind.

[2] Related by Imām Aḥmad, Ibn Ḥibbān and other authorities.

[3] Former anti-Islām Dutch politician, Arnoud van Doorn, converted to Islām in this very manner. He was a member of the far-right Freedom Party (PVV) and was involved in the production of derogatory, malicious, hate-filled anti-Islām propaganda. However, after extensive study about Islām and the Prophet (صَلَّى ٱللَّٰهُ عَلَيْهِ وَسَلَّمَ) he embraced Islām in 2013. His son, Iskander van Doorn, also accepted Islām in April 2014 after observing the profound effect Islām had on his father. This story echoes similar stories that took place during the call of the Prophet Muḥammad (صَلَّى ٱللَّٰهُ عَلَيْهِ وَسَلَّمَ). No sooner had people managed to

Islām, when the polytheists of Quraysh would mock and ridicule the Prophet (ﷺ) and use every means possible just to hinder the people from hearing his speech including propaganda, violence, torture and death. The disturbing events taking place these days - whether acts of terrorism or anti-Islām propaganda and violence towards its people - are simply a means amongst the means through which interest is being generated in the minds of inquisitive, thinking people about the teachings of Islām and the commotion regarding this intriguing man, Muḥammad (ﷺ). The man whose mockery, it seems, has been specifically designated as the ultimate "*test*" for the principle of *the freedom of speech.*

In this book, we aim to explore this issue in light of the recent attacks in Paris. Three central issues will be briefly mentioned here to set the context and a detailed elaboration will be made in what follows in the remainder of the book.

THE PROPHETS AND MESSENGERS OF GOD

The Prophets and Messengers of God - such as Abraham, Moses, all the Prophets of the Children of Isra'īl (Jacob), Jesus and the last of whom is Muḥammad (ﷺ) - came with a message of **instrinsic meaning, value, purpose** and **direction** for human life. They explained the 'why' and the 'purpose' and conveyed moral codes and laws founded upon

---

listen to the reality of his message except that they hastened to Islām. For that reason, the enemies of Muḥammad (ﷺ) thought he was bewitching the people. They could not fathom how people would instantaneously convert to Islām despite all the anti-Islām bias they had managed to spread. Today, we have a similar situation, except that the barriers are much greater and more sophisticated. The presence of mass media propaganda outlets, magazines, anti-Islām hate networks which are well-funded make it all the more difficult for the average person to see beyond the propaganda. Despite that however, information is readily available in a manner like never before and the person who sincerely desires to study Islām and the life of the Prophet Muḥammad (ﷺ) through objective, non-biased sources will see an altogether different picture than the one commonly portrayed.

this basis. Resurrection after death,[4] accountability in the hereafter and recompense for one's deeds justifies the affirmation of absolute morality and a right and wrong.[5] Without these affairs, there would be no objective basis for morality, no consistent sense of right and wrong and oppression, rights-violations, turmoil, mass-murder, destruction and pillage could be justified by individuals, governments and nations purely on grounds of self-interest, bought science or might is right.

THE PROPHETS OF EXISTENTIAL NIHILISM

Existential nihilism is the philosophical theory that *life has no intrinsic, inherent meaning or value*. This is stating that each and every human being or the entire human species is **insignificant** and **purposeless**. In this philosophy, each person is born with the impossibility of ever knowing the 'why' or the 'purpose' and will be compelled to create his or her own meaning in life. It is not inherently significant, meaningful or purposeful. Meaninglessness of life is the subject studied in the philosophy of existentialism and looks at how a person can create their own personal, subjective 'meaning' and 'purpose.'[6] There are various types of nihilism[7] but existential nihilism receives the most literary and philosophical attention. The revered prophets of this philosophy include **Jean-Paul Sartre** (French), **Albert Camus** (French), **Martin Heidegger** (German) and others. The idea of the absolute

[4] Evidence for the plausibility and occurrence of resurrection is all around us in the continuous cycles of life, death and rebirth in all living things.

[5] Thus, Hitler, Stalin and Mao Tse Tung and every other oppressor will be held accountable for their deeds.

[6] As did Hitler, Stalin, Mao Tse Tung and as does every small or large scale serial killer, rapist and embezzler.

[7] The peer reviewed Internet Encyclopedia of Philosophy defines nihilism as "The belief that all values are baseless and that nothing can be known or communicated. It is often associated with extreme pessimism and a radical skepticism that condemns existence." In the Merriam-Webster dictionary nihilism is defined as, "A doctrine that denies any objective ground of truth and especially of moral truths" and also "the belief that traditional morals, ideas, beliefs, etc., have no worth or value."

"*freedom of speech*" (as are many other values of modern society) is tied to the ideas of "*absence of meaning, significance and purpose*" and "*baselessness of values.*" Hence, no absolute values exist and nothing is therefore sacred, special or inviolable. Because nothing is inviolable, special or significant, one is potentially free to violate every sanctity in speech or deed. The inherent contradiction, futility (and hypocrisy) in this philosophy is known to all people of sound mind.[8]

FRENCH COURT RULINGS, CHARLIE HEBDO AND FREEDOM OF SPEECH

In March 2005, a French court judged that a clothing advertisement based on the "Last Supper" painting was "*a gratuitous and aggressive act of intrusion on people's innermost beliefs.*" Authorities in Italy had already banned the poster a month earlier. The poster was a female version of the "Last Supper" painting intended to promote designer clothing. The French judge ordered all posters to be taken down within three days. The Italian watchdog said that the use of Christian symbols including a dove and a chalice "*recalled the foundations of the faith and would offend the sensitivity of part of the population.*"[9] The designers, Marithe et Francois Girbaud, who made the advertisement appealed, saying that they did not intent to offend anyone with the campaign. A month later, the court upheld the ban.[10] The Paris appeals court said

[8] Upon this philosophy of subjective, personal (and not absolute) moral values, it is nothing but a matter of personal opinion between Hitler and the numerous ethnic minorities he mass-murdered or between Stalin and the 20 million mostly Christian peasants he wiped out or between the biggest mass-murderer in the 20th century, Mao Tse Tung, and the 50 million Chinese (at least) whom he annihilated. They all had arguments, *philosophical, scientific or otherwise*, to justify their evil activities. Atheistic and nihilistic philosophies cannot rationally and coherently refute these evil actions and judge them to be "absolutely" wrong in the overall scheme of purposelessness, baselessness of values and insignificance of life which are core foundational principles in these philosophies about existence, life and morality. Therefore, an atheist's moral judgements are just his or her personal opinions and hold as much weight as the air through which they are expressed.

[9] *French Court Bans Christ Advert*, BBC News, 11th March 2005.

[10] *French Christ Advert Ban Upheld*, BBC News, 8th April 2005.

that the display "*insults the religious feeling of Catholics.*" In February 2006, Charlie Hebdo reprinted cartoons of Prophet Muḥammad (صَلَّى ٱللَّٰهُ عَلَيْهِ وَسَلَّمَ) and were taken to court by Islāmic groups on the grounds of inciting hatred against Muslims. The editor, **Phillipe Val** was acquitted by the court which said that the cartoons were covered by freedom of expression laws. The case was seen as **an important test for freedom of expression** in France.[11] Applause broke out in the court when the verdict was announced and it ruled that the three cartoons were not insulting to the Muslim community.[12] The editor, Phillipe Val, said that the cartoons were not an attack on Muslims, but on terrorists.[13] Then in 2009, Maurice Sinet, a columnist for Charlie Hebdo was asked to apologise by **Phillipe Val** for making an anti-semitic jibe at Jean Sarkozy, son of the President, Nicolas, by remarking "*He'll go a long way in life he will, that little lad*" because of his marriage to a successful Jewish businesswoman. Controversy arose because of complaints about the column from a political commentator. **When Sinet refused to leave he was fired by Phillipe Val who considered the remark to be *offensive*.** He was later taken to court and put to trial on charges of anti-semitism and inciting racial hatred by a group known as Licra.[14] When we consider that until 2013 insulting the French president was a criminal offence[15] and that an Algerian man was fined for insulting

[11] It is very revealing that of all things, mocking the Prophet Muhammad (صَلَّى ٱللَّٰهُ عَلَيْهِ وَسَلَّمَ) has become *the* important test for the freedom of expression.

[12] Meaning, *the court decided* whether the Muslims felt insulted or not. That they actually did, had no bearing at all.

[13] Terrorists can be attacked and refuted for their evil without offending 1.5 billion people (a quarter of the planet) through calculated provocation. Especially when the basis of this mockery is false. The Prophet of Islām has extremely harsh words about those very same terrorists in his traditions as is famous and well-known to the Scholars of Islām and learned Muslims (see the examples later in this book).

[14] *French Cartoonist Sine on Trial on Charges of Anti-Semitism over Sarkozy Jibe* in the Telegraph, 27th Jan 2009.

[15] A man was convicted of a criminal offence in 2008 for holding up a card saying, "Get lost, you prat" as Sarkozy's motorcade passed by during a presidential visit to Laval in western France. The same remark was actually made by Sarkozy earlier in the year to a man in a crowd who refused to shake

the French flag in 2010[16] and many other similar examples that have been brought to light recently, one might surmise that latent prejudices against Muslims might be interfering with the way in which the alleged right of freedom of expression and the right to offend are allowed to be exercised.

What follows in this book was originally a series of writings sent out via Twitter over a period of three days (between 12th-14th January) after the events of 7th-10th January 2015 in Paris, France with the aim of defending and exonerating the Prophet of Islām (ﷺ) from two parties that attribute to him that which he is free and innocent of: **The Khārijite**[17] **terrorist savages** on the one hand who justify murder and carnage which Islām has outlawed and **the atheistic existentialist nihilists** and their likes on the other hand who spread lies and slanders justified by the alleged right of *absolute* freedom of speech.[18] To make the book of more benefit for inquisitive non-Muslims, I have included a concise presentation of the foundational teaching of Islām towards the early part of the book.[19]

Abu Iyaaḍ

9th Rabī al-Thānī 1436 / 29th January 2015

Sarkozy's hand. *Why French Law Treats Dieudonné and Charlie Hebdo Differently*, New Yorker Magazine, 15th January 2015.

[16] *Man fined for insulting French flag*, BBC, 23rd December 2010.

[17] The word *Khārijite* means renegade and refers to a group who were prophesized by Muḥammad (ﷺ) to appear recurringly throughout the ages against the Muslims, putting them through trials and tribulations.

[18] No serious Western philosopher actually believes in the plausibility of such a concept neither in theory nor in practice. The relevant laws of most countries will confirm this, not least the laws in many European nations which make illegal and prohibit, through threat of huge fines and imprisonment, the scrutinization of claims about historical events even from a *purely neutral, academic* perspective.

[19] I would like to thank Ḥasan al-Sumālī, Abū Ḥakīm Bilāl Davis, Abū Khadījah ʿAbd al-Wāḥid, Abdulilāh Lahmāmi, Abū Tasnīm Muṣhaf, Bilāl Ḥussain, ʿUways Tawīl and others who reviewed the book in its various stages, offered useful suggestions, corrected typographical errors, gave constructive advice and were supportive of the project.

A Condemnation of the Terrorist Acts

First and foremost, as much as Muslims deplore mockery of the Prophet (صَلَّى ٱللَّٰهُ عَلَيْهِ وَسَلَّمَ), find it very offensive and consider it to be motivated by spite and hate before it is motivated by the alleged fallacious claim of the *absolute* freedom to express one's opinion, the actions which took place in France between 7th-10th January 2015 are still unlawful in the Islāmic Sharīʿah. This is because issues of this nature and gravity are only dealt with by Islāmic governments and not young, ignorant fools intoxicated by an evil, extremist ideology, who take up arms, kill innocent people, terrorize society and bring greater harm upon Muslims in every place. The Salafī scholar, Shaykh ʿUbayd al-Jābirī, of al-Madīnah (KSA) was asked the following question on 9th January 2015:[20]

Questioner: "A couple of days ago a number of cartoonists who behaved maliciously towards the noble Messenger (صَلَّى ٱللَّٰهُ عَلَيْهِ وَسَلَّمَ) and some journalists and employees who worked for Charlie Hebdo in Paris were killed. Likewise, two men and a woman from the police were also killed. Until now, the perpetrators of these criminal acts have not been apprehended. However, some video clips have appeared in which there is glorification of one of the criminals and their saying that they committed this action - as they claim - out of revenge for the noble Messenger (صَلَّى ٱللَّٰهُ عَلَيْهِ وَسَلَّمَ). As a result, fingers are now being pointed towards Islām and the Muslims in general and towards the Muslims who live in France specifically. Fires have been set alight and bombs have been hurled at some of the mosques. So the question is - may Allāh protect you: What is the position of the Salafī towards these terrorist actions[21] and what is your advice to the

---

[20] The question was posed by Salafī Muslims seeking scholarly guidance and advice on the matter and the answer was subsequently published online and distributed through social media.

[21] The Salafīs and their scholars have always been at the forefront of refuting and warning against terrorists because this type of extremism fundamentally clashes with the very foundations of pure, orthodox Islām and is behind the

Muslims of France and to the Salafī callers more specifically? May Allāh reward you with good."

Shaykh 'Ubayd al-Jābirī responded with the following comments and advice: "**Firstly**, there is no person who follows the Sunnah[22] whose heart has not been tarnished with innovated heresies - regardless of whether he is a scholar or a competent student of knowledge or he is from the students of knowledge less than them or a common person who sits with the scholars and their students - except that **he rejects these [criminal] actions** whether they occur at [the likes of] this newspaper or others besides it and how numerous are [such newspapers]. **Secondly**, all the intelligent people from the Jews and Christians who have lived side by side with the Muslims in their lands recognize this. Even those [politicians] with major [positions of] responsibility in the European states, America and elsewhere feel safe and at ease with the people who follow the Sunnah and Jamā'ah,[23] they feel at ease and safe with the Salafīs.[24]

---

emergence of the very first sect in Islām, the Khārijite renegades who revolted against the Prophet's Companions (رَضِيَ اللَّهُ عَنْهُمْ), excommunicated them, fought against them and killed the best of them. Hence, this evil ideology is a war against Islām and its people before it is a war against anyone else.

[22] The "Sunnah" is the way of the Prophet Muḥammad (ﷺ) and represents the sum of what he practiced, in speech and deed and has been preserved through a rigorous, scientific methodology that has no precedence in history in the field of oral and written transmission.

[23] Those who remain steadfast and united as a single body upon orthodox Islāmic teachings.

[24] Genuine, orthodox Salafī Muslims should not be confused with the **Muslim Brotherhood**, **Hizb al-Taḥrīr** (and its camouflaged offshoots), **al-Qā'idah** or **ISIS** Khārijites and terrorists who hijack the label and identity of "Salafiyyah" as a means of camouflaging their evil ideology. These extremists have been consistently and efficiently refuted and exposed by the Salafīs over the last 20 years at least. This false ascription to Salafiyyah on their behalf is merely a stratagem to acquire legitimacy and to tarnish the image of the very Salafīs to whom they are avowed enemies. One should also not be deceived by academics and journalists who perpetuate this confusion, whether due to ignorance or deliberate intent, by not distinguishing between Salafī Muslims and the Takfīrī Jihādīsts or the Khārijites in general, violent or non-violent.

Thirdly, it has thus become clear from what has preceded that it is not permissible for these [criminal] actions to be ascribed to the person who is upon the Sunnah. **Rather, they emanate from the Khārijites, the scum, the savages and the anarchists.** In some cases, these anarchists are Rāfiḍah[25] and in some cases they are non-Muslims who wear the gown of Muslims [pretending to be Muslims][26] who plant themselves amongst the Rāfiḍah or the Khārijites from the fanatics amongst the Muslim Brotherhood and others besides them. For the group of the Muslim Brotherhood[27] - which is one of the recently-arisen groups involved in making an Islāmic call and all of these [newly-arisen groups] are misguided and misguide others - they

[25] The term "Rāfiḍah" (Rejectors) refers to the Shīʿites who display enmity towards the Prophet's Companions (رَضِيَ ٱللَّهُ عَنْهُمْ) and consider Sunnī Muslims to be apostates. From their core doctrines is the belief that an awaited Mahdī (leader) is to appear who will lead them against Sunnī Muslims, annihilate them and take over their lands including the cities of Makkah and al-Madīnah. It is not uncommon for Shīʿite proxy communities in Sunnī lands to create strife and commotion as a means of paving the way for revolutions which they believe will hasten the appearance of the alleged Mahdī.

[26] In light of research performed into *entrapment*, not all planned, failed or successful acts of terrorism in non-Muslim lands may actually be perpetrated by Muslims. Refer to "*The Informants*" by Trevor Aaronson in the September 2011 issue of Mother Jones magazine (available online). There is also Stephen Down and Kathy Manley's detailed 178-page academic study titled, "*Inventing Terrorists: The Lawfare of Preemptive Prosecution*" and a search for "Muslim entrapment" will return many examples of media coverage on this subject. However, this cannot and must not be used to downplay the actual terrorism perpetrated by the Khārijite extremists. **Khārijites were not created by any foreign policy of any Western nation. This is a fallacy used by terrorist sympathizers to excuse their evil actions.** Rather, they have existed for 1400 years and have been putting Islām and the Muslims to trial in all that time. Most non-Muslims will be unaware of these historical facts and of the abundant statements of the Prophet (ﷺ) regarding them and their evil. These statements are presented later in the book.

[27] The main ideological figureheads of the Muslim Brotherhood such as Ḥasan al-Bannā and Sayyid Quṭb are responsible for creating and spreading the doctrines which led to the birth of extremist Takfīrī and Jihādī groups like al-Qaidah and ISIS. They came from the Ṣūfī, Ashʿarī tradition and were not Salafī Muslims, neither in belief nor in methodology.

declare it permissible to seek the assistance of non-Muslims for what they desire of political [goals].

Thus, it is not far-fetched [to say] that this [criminal] act may have been perpetrated in order to cause injury to the people who follow the Sunnah specifically and to [cause injury] to the Muslims who reside in France and the [countries] besides it from the European and American states. [This act may have been done] so that commotion can be raised against the people who follow the Sunnah, specifically. In concluding this speech I advise our sons, the Salafīs, in whichever land they are found, whether in France specifically or in other than it from the European, American and African states, in the non-Muslim countries, I advise the [imāms] who give sermons, the teachers, the lecturers and Muslim journalists to unite upon a single word and it is: **To openly announce [their] disavowal and innocence from this action and other actions of anarchy.** The people of the Sunnah are those who safeguard their agreements and their fulfilment of them. The people of the Sunnah are the people who implement the [terms] of their agreements. The people of the Sunnah protect their neighbours, they maintain the honour of the neighbour. They do not transgress his honour, nor against his wealth nor against his person.

The people of the Sunnah hold it as their religion before Allāh that in the lands of Europe, America and other non-Muslim lands besides them in which they have settled there is a covenant, a contract. Hence, they must not violate it [through treachery], ever.[28]

[28] The late Salafī Scholar, Shaykh Muḥammad bin Ṣāliḥ al-ʿUthaymīn of Saudi Arabia stated, during a tele-link in the evening of Friday, 28th July 2000, to an audience in the city of Birmingham, UK, during a conference organized by Salafi Publications: "Likewise I invite you to have respect for those people who have the right that they should be respected, those between whom there is an agreement (of protection) for you. For the land in which you are living is such that there is an agreement between you and them. If this were not the case they would have killed you or expelled you. So preserve this agreement, and do not prove treacherous to it, since treachery is a sign of the Hypocrites, and it is not from the way of the Believers."

As I have already stated, the intelligent amongst the Jews, Christians and others respect the Salafīs and feel at ease and safe with the people who follow the Sunnah and they know that this [criminal action] has not come from them.[29] There remains [the issue] of the explosion of bombs at the mosques. I do not consider it far-fetched, in fact, I am certain that it was deliberate harm which may have been from the group of the political Muslim Brotherhood or it may have been from unintelligent non-Muslim maniacs.[30] This is what I advise and affirm with respect to this criminal act and Allāh is the One who bestows success." End of the statement of Shaykh ʿUbayd al-Jābirī.[31]

---

[29] Such reasonable, objective and intelligent people from the non-Muslims who are plentiful in number are genuinely and sincerely thanked.

[30] A befitting description. How can such people abhor terrorism and then go on to perpetrate it against a people who are equally its victims and abhor it just as much as they do? This establishes that extremist right-wing groups who harm or even kill Muslims are just as evil as the Khārijite terrorists and shows that they do not operate upon any principles or values in reality.

[31] Another scholar from the city of al-Madīnah, Shaykh ʿAbdullāh al-Bukhārī, also offered some advice days later on the same matter. His advice can be summarized in the following broad points: **First**, that these tribulations are the direct result of the spread of ignorance and the lack of correct Sharīʿah knowledge. All tribulations occur due to opposition to what the Prophet Muḥammad (صَلَّى ٱللَّٰهُ عَلَيْهِ وَسَلَّمَ) came with and this event in Paris and others like it are a manifestation of that. **Second**, it is an individual obligation upon all Muslims to take knowledge directly from genuine, bona fide, orthodox scholars of the Prophetic traditions and not from ignoramuses, mischief-makers and opposers. Then they must act upon this knowledge, putting it into practice so its fruits can be attained. **Third**, The Messenger laid down ways and paths of rectification. That which is done in opposition to them cannot be ascribed to Islām and Islām is free of it. A Muslim must free himself from every affair which opposes the truth just like the Companion ʿAbdullāh bin ʿUmar (رَضِيَ ٱللَّٰهُ عَنْهُ) freed himself from the deviants who appeared in Irāq in his time as soon as he was informed of their deviation and opposition to what the Prophet (صَلَّى ٱللَّٰهُ عَلَيْهِ وَسَلَّمَ) came with. **Fourth**, every person who is pleased with Allāh as his Lord, Islām as his religion and Muḥammad as his Messenger must support Islām and aid the Messenger by implementing his teachings and following his Sunnah. This is how the Messenger is aided. **Fifth**, violating contracts and acting with perfidy and treachery is not from the traits of the Believers, it is the trait of the Hypocrites. The Prophet Muḥammad

Shaykh ʿUbayd al-Jābirī has echoed a consistent viewpoint that has been known amongst well-known and prominent Salafī scholars: To enjoin upon all Muslims in every place to openly disavow these actions of terrorism and anarchy. Condemnation of such actions is a test for identifying any terrorist sympathizer. The one who hesitates in condemning what is unlawful in the Islāmic Sharīʿah, namely to hijack public places, kill innocent people, both Muslims and non-Muslims without discrimination, to terrorize the society and disrupt public life, then it is known by necessity that he has a disease in his heart and inwardly validates these types of disgraceful actions. From such terrorist sympathizers and misguided deviants are the likes of Anjem Choudary[32] who, very sadly, are given airtime on mass media and allowed to spread lies, misconceptions and distortions about Islām in front of tens of millions. Thus, it is upon all Muslims to disavow these actions and warn against the terrorist criminals, their sympathizers and those who glorify their evil actions.

Once the Islāmic position regarding this act of terrorism has been made clear, let us take a look at the essential message of Islām which may not be apparent to many non-Muslims or misunderstood by them due to the many doubts which are spread. Thereafter, we will address the person of the Prophet Muḥammad (صَلَّى ٱللَّٰهُ عَلَيْهِ وَسَلَّمَ) and evaluate the lies and insults directed at him.

(صَلَّى ٱللَّٰهُ عَلَيْهِ وَسَلَّمَ) mentioned the traits of hypocrisy and amongst them is breaking promises and being treacherous to one's covenant. **Sixth**, that which was done in Paris is rejected by the Sharīʿah and these acts were done by ignoramuses. These actions bring harm upon the Muslims and contain no benefit. **Seventh**, those who follow the Sunnah should fulfil their covenant (mīthāq) in whichever place they live and if they desire to defend the religion it should be done with the truth, not with falsehood. The followers of the Sunnah are free of these evil actions.

[32] Anjem Choudary is a follower of the ideology of Taqī al-Dīn al-Nabhānī, the founder of Hizb al-Taḥrīr, a former Baʿthist Communist who was involved in nationalist movements in the late 1940s.

The Essence of Islām: The Way of the Prophets

The following narrative conveys the essence of Islām: The most basic of observations of the universe whether at large or small (quantum) scales indicates an underlying order and regularity. Through complex interwoven, interdependent laws, the universe and all atoms and particles therein are in a state of submission.[33] The fundamental assumption behind all scientific observation, analysis and inquiry - without which it cannot take place - is the **design**, **order**, **regularity** and **rational investigability** of this universe. No scientific paper which has ever been written on the "natural" world is devoid of language that implies design. Not even an atheist can escape the use of language and terminology which assumes design in what is being studied and described.[34] The claim of design being "illusory" is arrogation in the face of the obvious and is a conclusion demanded by a prior conviction in materialism. Being able to observe and analyze the world around us, to make rational sense of it and the ability to innovate in many ways, industrially, technologically, biologically and biotechnologically through the understanding so acquired is from the greatest of evidences of design in life and the universe.[35] This leads,

---

[33] This is known as *al-ʿubūdiyyah al-kawniyyah* (universal submission) which nothing can escape. Atheist astronomers and astrophysicists admit that the *impression of design* is overwhelming due to the many symmetries and extremely fine, delicate balances in the universe but prior conviction and commitment to materialism forces them to attribute design to "nature."

[34] Refer to *Humans may be primed to believe in creation*, New Scientist (29th February 2009). The researchers noted that even highly-renowned scientists such as Einstein or Dawkins would not be able to escape "the tendency to fall back upon teleological explanations," meaning, purposeful design.

[35] Materialism as a philosophy is not proven by science, but is an assumed starting point on the basis of which the conclusions of science are kept within psychologically comfortable limits for sufferers of ***cosmic authority syndrome*** which is a dislike of the idea that there should be an authority over the universe at all. It is this emotion in reality, not the mechanism of science, which drove atheistic philosophies in the West after great discontentment with the Church. Islām, in which sound, uncorrupted reason does not conflict with revelation as a matter of principle, never had this experience.

through only the shortest of logical and rational steps, to a designer and maker.[36] In Islāmic terminology, this acknowledgement is part of an inherent, innate faculty (referred to as the ***fiṭrah***) which every child is born with. Research indicates that all children are primed to believe in a Creator.[37] Each child is born predisposed to affirming a Creator who is perceived through only the most basic of observations to own and regulate the universe through an intricate, intertwined system of elements, forces, causes and effects.[38] If left alone, without any instruction or contrary teaching, every child will develop with a compelling desire to show gratitude to this Creator for the favours and bounties experienced and enjoyed in life.[39]

---

[36] Atheists like Richard Dawkins acknowledge this is a compelling, rational argument which cannot be easily refuted. Thus, the only response is to posit **an alternative *competing* explanation** for the "apparent" design in life and the universe. However, this competing explanation is **exclusively demanded** by a *prior conviction* in materialist philosophy, but not at the same time **demanded exclusively** by objective scientific inquiry.

[37] Based on research at Oxford University by Justin Barrett and Olivera Petrovich and refer also to *Humans may be primed to believe in creation*, New Scientist (29th February 2009) and *Children Are Born Believers in God*, Daily Telegraph (24th November 2008).

[38] The only other possibilities being **self-creation**, as in the universe created itself, a clear impossibility or **creation *by nothing***, meaning, it came to be after not being without the intervention of any other entity or cause, hence, nothing brought it about and it therefore escaped **the universal law of causality** (*every material effect must have an adequate antecedent cause*), the ultimate canon of all sciences. This event was then followed by random, non-purposeful, undirected, self-organization of matter until it became dust, water, DNA, cells, plants, trees, animals, Senator Al Gore and the Internet. This is **a positively asserted conjectural belief system** built upon a prior commitment to materialism. This explanation of the universe is considered true *because* materialism, as a belief system, has been asserted to be true before any science has taken place. Science is then defined and conducted in a manner to keep its findings within this belief system in order to protect and maintain the world-view built upon it.

[39] Even atheists admit of experiencing this compelling impulse. In his Fixed-Point debate at the University of Alabama (2007), Richard Dawkins admitted, "I think that when you consider the beauty of the world and you wonder how it came to be what it is, you are naturally overwhelmed with a feeling of awe,

THE CALL OF THE MESSENGERS

In light of this, the Messengers such as Abraham, Moses, Jesus and Muḥammad (صَلَّىٰ اللَّهُ عَلَيْهِ وَسَلَّمَ) were *not* sent to invite people to affirm a Creator as it is already an innate, rationally justified and warranted belief. The vast majority of people in human history have never denied a supreme creator in one form or another. Rather, the Messengers were sent with a rational necessity (*ḍurūrah*) demanded by the **innate disposition** (*fitrah*) and justified through **sound reason** (*ʿaql*) which is to show devotion and gratitude to this Creator *alone* for the innumerable bounties and favours that one enjoys on a daily basis. This is **monotheism (Tawḥīd)**, the core message of Noah, Abraham, Moses, Jesus (عَلَيْهِمُ السَّلَامُ) and Muḥammad (صَلَّىٰ اللَّهُ عَلَيْهِ وَسَلَّمَ). This monotheism is **the foundation of Islām** which linguistically means *to submit*. Legislatively, it means to submit to the Creator alone in pure

---

a feeling of admiration and you almost feel a desire to worship something. I feel this, I recognise that other scientists such as Carl Sagan feel this, Einstein felt it. We, all of us, share a kind of religious reverence for the beauties of the universe, for the complexity of life. For the sheer magnitude of the cosmos, the sheer magnitude of geological time. And it's tempting to translate that feeling of awe and worship into a desire to worship some particular thing, a person, an agent. You want to attribute it to a maker, to a creator." However, what drives atheists like Dawkins is the mental condition of *cosmic authority syndrome*. They do not like the idea of a universe with an authority over it. Intelligent, honest atheists such as famous evolutionary biologist Richard Lewontin, philosopher Thomas Nagel and others admit that science does not compel a materialist explanation of life and that atheism is simply a psychologically preferred world view. An atheist does not want God to exist and feels more comfortable emotionally without belief in God. This is the actual starting point. Science and its mechanisms come afterwards. The claim that science has proved materialism and eliminated the need for a creator is sophistry in reason. This is because science is specifically defined to avoid discussions of *origins* and *final goals* of cause-effect systems and to maintain focus on purely material descriptions of cause-effect systems. Hence, out-of-realm conclusions or metaphysical claims such as "*God does not exist*" cannot be made through the scientific method so defined. Honest atheists (such as Lewontin, Nagel and others) understand this well and are unafraid to admit it. Blind-following atheists who lack honesty are not.

monotheism in speech and deed. In addition to innate disposition (*fiṭrah*), man has been bestowed with **intellect** (*ʿaql*) which is the ability to reason, **wish** (*irādah*) which is the ability to choose and finally, **ability** (*qudrah*) which is the capacity to act. These faculties justify **human responsibility** (*taklīf*) and subsequent accounting and recompense for one's deeds. However, accountability is justified not on the basis of any innate faculty or reason but only after revelation has been sent. In other words, reward and punishment only apply once the message of the Prophets has reached a person. Allāh (عَزَّوَجَلَّ) said, "**And never would we punish (a people) until we have sent a messenger.**" (17:15). This is because the evidence of reason is inadequate in answering the question of 'why' and 'purpose' and any observation, theorization, philosophical thought or scientific inquiry is only ever built upon prior assumptions which make its truth-reaching capacity limited and impaired. For this reason, philosophers and scientists cannot and never will answer the ultimate questions regarding existence and life. Their speculations cannot offer true guidance regarding the purpose of life. In contrast to the Prophets and Messengers whose core message is uniform and consistent, the philosophers and scientists are at variance with each other and do not have a united word in these affairs indicating the conjectural nature of what they profess.

Hence, the central doctrine of pure monotheism which comprises the foundation of Islām is considered - in the message of all of the Prophets such as Abraham, Moses, Jesus and Muḥammad (صَلَّى اللَّهُ عَلَيْهِ وَسَلَّمَ) - to be the truth (*ḥaqq*) and justice (*ʿadl*) upon which the Heavens and Earth were created, upon which they exist and upon which they run their course and are governed. Therefore, offering devotion and gratitude to this Creator alone for the innumerable favours, bounties and enjoyments one experiences in life is from the greatest justice (*ʿadl*). Whoever abides by this has established the justice which the Heavens and Earth were founded upon. True peace of mind, serenity and satisfaction naturally follow. And whoever violated this intuitive, rational necessity has committed the greatest injustice (*ẓulm*) which is known as associationism (*shirk*). As for the name of this creator, it is Allāh (*īl, el, ilāh, iloh, elah*) in the languages of Aramaic, Hebrew and Arabic. This is not "*the God of the Muslims*" but rather the God of all the Prophets, of all nations and of all humanity.

ALL MANKIND WAS ONCE UNITED UPON ISLĀM

Allāh (عَزَّوَجَلَّ) said, "**He has ordained for you of religion what He enjoined upon Noah and that which We have revealed to you, [O Muḥammad], and what We enjoined upon Abraham and Moses and Jesus.**" (42:13). Islām was the message of Noah, Abraham, Moses, all the Prophets of the Children of Isrā'īl (Jacob) including Solomon, David and also that of Jesus, John and finally, Muḥammad (ﷺ). Mankind was once united upon Islām. Allāh (عَزَّوَجَلَّ) said, "**Mankind was [of] one religion [before their deviation], then Allāh sent the prophets as bringers of good tidings and warners and sent down with them the Scripture in truth to judge between the people concerning that in which they differed.** (2:213). It is the very nature of *tawḥīd* (monotheism) and Islām to unite mankind irrespective of race, culture, status or class. Allāh (عَزَّوَجَلَّ) said, "**And We did not send any messenger except with the language of his people to explain clearly to them.**" (14:3). Every messenger expressed the same meanings comprised in the words *salām* (peace), *islām* (submission), *muslim* (submitter) and *tawḥīd* (monotheism) in his respective language. From this perspective, the Prophets are considered brothers with an identical message. The Companion, Abū Hurayrah (رَضِيَ ٱللَّهُ عَنْهُ) reported that the Prophet (ﷺ) said, "*Both in this world and in the Hereafter, I am the nearest of all the people to Jesus, the son of Mary. The prophets are paternal brothers, their mothers are different, but their religion is one.*"[40] Whoever grasps the above will perceive the capacity of this simple, powerful and compelling message to unite mankind.[41]

---

[40] Related by Imām al-Bukhārī in his compilation of Prophetic traditions.

[41] Islām acknowledges cultural diversity, the variant habits of people and their customs so long as they do not comprise falsehood, oppression, harm or moral corruption.

Throughout history, people deviated from innate disposition (*fiṭrah*), sound reason (*ʿaql*) and the message of the Prophets (*risālah*) and began to to give others a share in the devotion that is due rightfully only to Allāh. The worship of others - be they humans, the Jinn, the Angels, the planetary bodies including the Earth, Sun and Moon, the elements, trees, stones, even the Prophets themselves or the righteous living or dead or the elements and forces - is the greatest injustice (*ẓulm*). In Islāmic terminology it is referred to as associationism (*shirk*). It is a violation of the truth upon which the universe stands and persists.[42] This is because the worship of others besides or alongside the sole, unique creator is built upon assumptions whose futility are apparent in basic reason. These assumptions are: That the thing worshipped owns or shares in the ownership of all or part of creation or that the thing worshipped is a helper to the Creator in regulating His creation or that the thing worshipped has independent control over benefit and harm or that the thing worshipped can forgive and accept repentance and what is similar to that. Since these are false assumptions for created entities, elements, forces and all causes and effects, then venerating them and worshipping them exclusively or alongside the Creator is falsehood. It is a deviation from innate disposition (*fiṭrah*), a revilement of reason and comprises the greatest injustice. This crime of associationism (*shirk*) is more unjust than stealing, murder, adultery and other such moral transgressions. This can be highlighted through the example of a person who shows gratitude and devotion to a brick or a mouse or a cat for the many years of toil and struggle that his parents endured in raising him.[43] This is gross injustice. In a similar way, worshipping

---

[42] An astounding number of intertwined, harmonious systems of cause and effect bear witness to the originator of these causes and effects who must be external to the sum of them and can never be part of them. Thus, it is futile to worship parts of the creation (such as planetary bodies, humans and the elements) or any of the innumerable causes or their effects. This comprises revilement of reason and deviation from innate disposition.

[43] This is not to imply that the Creator of the Heavens and the Earth becomes weary or tired in maintaining and providing for His creatures. He (عَزَّوَجَلَّ) said regarding the Heavens and Earth, "**Their preservation tires Him not. And He**

humans, animals, the forces, the elements or anything from the intertwined system of causes and effects within this universe is gross injustice. It opposes innate disposition and comprises revilement of sound intellect.

The Messengers came to call the people to abandon false worship, declaring it to be the greatest injustice (*ẓulm*). Hence, the essence of their call was to single out Allāh in worship and to shun all false deities. Allāh (عَزَّوَجَلَّ) said, "**And We certainly sent into every nation a messenger, [saying]: Worship Allāh (alone) and avoid false deities.**" (16:36). False deities are numerous and are defined as anything worshipped besides the Creator or with respect to which the limits are transgressed in worship, following and obedience. Rejecting false dieties and singling out Allāh in worship is the essential foundation and pillar of Islām and every Prophet called to it. It is embodied in the declaration of faith which every messenger proclaimed, "*There is none worthy and deserving of worship [in truth] except Allāh alone.*" Whoever affirms this belief has abided by the order and justice upon which the universe stands and whoever acted upon the necessities of this belief, man or woman, is guaranteed Paradise.[44] This foundational belief necessitates other beliefs which follow on from it such as belief in all the Messengers without distinction, belief in all the revealed Books sent by Allāh, belief in the Resurrection and the Day of Judgement, the belief that everything in creation is by due measure (*qadar*) and belief in unseen matters of which we have been informed through revelation but whose knowledge is inaccessible to sensory perception or reason.

---

is the Most High, the Most Great" (2:255). Allāh (عَزَّوَجَلَّ) provides and spends upon His creatures without anything diminishing from His kingdom and without any tiredness or weariness on His behalf, He is the ever-living (al-Ḥayy) sustainer (al-Qayyūm) of all things. Nothing is diminished from His dominion by providing for His creatures.

[44] Thus, the Prophet Muḥammad (ﷺ) explained, "*Whoever dies without associating anything with Allāh [in worship] will enter Paradise.*" Related by al-Bukhārī in Kitāb al-Janāʾiz (no. 1238).

Diverse religions arose through opposition to innate disposition, opposition to sound reason and deviation from the message of the Prophets. When a religion is founded upon worship of other than Allāh or is named exclusively after an individual - a prophet or otherwise - or after a race,[45] or after an element amongst the elements or a force amongst the forces, or a cause amongst the causes or an effect amongst the effects, or any part of what is referred to as *nature*, it is known not to have come from Allāh and is a contrivance, an invention of the human mind. Besides the name of *Islām*, the names of all religions are contrived and invented and do not reflect the true, original message of pure monotheism (*Tawḥīd*) and submission (*Islām*) which every Prophet came with and they are in violation - in their doctrinal formulations - of the order, regularity, balance, truth and justice upon which the universe stands and persists. Thus, Abraham was a Muslim - meaning one who submitted to the will of the sole Creator, Owner and Regulator of this universe. Moses was a Muslim, as were all the Prophets of the Children of Israel (Banī Isrā᾽īl) including Solomon and David. Jesus and John were also Muslims and Islām was the name of their religion.

This is also known from the Aramaic (Syriac) and Hebrew languages which are similar to Arabic and comprise words identical to *salām* (peace), *islām* (submission) and *muslim* (submitter) which characterize the way acceptable to Allāh, **"Verily, the way (of life) in the sight of Allāh is Islām."** (3:19). The name Allāh is a contraction of two parts, the definite article *al* and the noun *ilāh*, meaning deity, which is also found in Hebrew and Aramaic (Syriac) as *iloh* or *elah*. Hence, the name of the creator is Allāh (the deity in truth) and Islām (submission to His

[45] Any religion or way that is based upon class discrimination, tribalism or is exclusive to a race or ethnicity is known automatically not to have come from Allāh (عَزَّ وَجَلَّ) or may be a distortion of what originally came from Allāh. This is because all humans are accountable and responsible and the message ought to be attainable for every person. The message of Islām is simple, intuitive, natural and human disposition is already inclined towards it. With the exception of Muḥammad (صَلَّىٰ ٱللَّٰهُ عَلَيْهِ وَسَلَّمَ), the message of all previous Prophets was localized and not intended to be universal.

will) was the message and way of all of His Prophets. This way of humble submission follows naturally from the submission of the entire universe to a will that is beyond it.[46] Every nation received a messenger at some point in its history who proclaimed this message. The simplicity of this message appeals naturally to every soul in the absence of arrogance, corrupt reasoning or following desires in which precedence is given to worldly pleasures, pursuits and allurements over the truth.[47] Those who felt threatened by the message resorted to jest and mockery amongst other things. Mockery of the Messengers is nothing new and every Messenger was subject to it. Allāh (عَزَّوَجَلَّ) stated in His Book, the Qurʾān, "**How regretful for the servants. There did not come to them any messenger except that they used to ridicule him.**" (36:30). He also said, "**And already were messengers ridiculed before you, but those who mocked them were enveloped by what they used to ridicule.**" (21:41). Once the essential message of Islām has been made clear, we can take a look at Muḥammad (ﷺ), the last and final Messenger of Allāh, and make sense of the reasons behind the continued attempts to mock, ridicule and dishonour him.

---

[46] Hence, the command to observe and reflect upon the universe and what it contains of wonders, marvels, order and harmony is frequent in the Qurʾān. This leads to an inevitable conclusion that there is a will behind it and that it has not been created in vain or without purpose, "**Say: 'Observe and reflect upon what is in the Heavens and Earth.' But of no avail will be signs or warners to a people who do not believe.**" (10:101) and "**Indeed, in the creation of the Heavens and the Earth and the alternation of the night and the day are signs for those of understanding. Those who remember Allāh while standing or sitting or [lying] on their sides and give thought to the creation of the Heavens and the Earth, [saying], 'Our Lord, You did not create this without purpose. Exalted are You [above such a thing]. Thus, protect us from the punishment of the Fire'.**" (3:190-191).

[47] The Christian Byzantine Emperor, Heraclius (d. 641CE), recognized and acknowledged that Muḥammad (ﷺ) was a true Prophet of God but fear of his ministers and subjects prevented him from accepting his message. Heraclius determined through Abū Sufyān, the leader of the tribe of Quraysh who at the time was still a non-Muslim and who had been summoned to his court, that Muḥammad (ﷺ) was a genuine Prophet. This incident is detailed by Imām al-Bukhārī in his famous collection of Prophetic traditions.

Muḥammad (صَلَّى ٱللَّهُ عَلَيْهِ وَسَلَّمَ): His Lofty Standard of Character

Allāh (عَزَّوَجَلَّ) stated in what He revealed to Muḥammad (صَلَّى ٱللَّهُ عَلَيْهِ وَسَلَّمَ):

وَإِنَّكَ لَعَلَىٰ خُلُقٍ عَظِيمٍ

And you are indeed upon a lofty standard of character. (68:4)

Muḥammad[48] (صَلَّى ٱللَّهُ عَلَيْهِ وَسَلَّمَ) is the son of ʿAbdullāh, the son of ʿAbd al-Muṭṭālib, the son of Hāshim and his lineage traces back, through 21 generations, to ʿAdnān who was from the offspring of Ismāʿīl, the son of Abraham. His mother was called Āminah, and her genealogy meets with that of her husband, ʿAbdullāh, at the fifth ancestor, Kilāb bin Murrah. Hence, the Prophetic genealogy traces back to Abraham through both routes and is an indication of the nobility of his lineage. He is mentioned in the Hebrew Torah as "Muḥammad" and in the Aramaic (Syriac) Gospel as "Ahmad." Allāh (سُبْحَانَهُ وَتَعَالَىٰ) said, **"Those to whom We gave the Scripture know him as they know their own sons. But indeed, a party of them conceal the truth while they know [it]."** (2:146). Due to their deep and firm knowledge of the scripture, many of the People of the Book, were anticipating a Prophet and moved to the areas surrounding Yathrib. This later became known as al-Madīnah al-Nabawiyyah (the City of the Prophet) when Muḥammad (صَلَّى ٱللَّهُ عَلَيْهِ وَسَلَّمَ) emigrated there after being forced to flee from persecution in Makkah. Allāh (سُبْحَانَهُ وَتَعَالَىٰ) said, **"And [mention] when Jesus, the son of Mary, said, 'O Children of Isrāʾīl, indeed I am the Messenger of Allāh to you confirming what came before me of the Torah and bringing good tidings of a messenger to come after me, whose name is Aḥmad.' But when he came to them with clear evidences, they said, 'This is obvious magic'."** (61:6). Many of the People of the Book accepted Islām and

[48] The name 'Muḥammad' means *the praised one* and as a matter of fact he is the most praised person on Earth which indicates the truthfulness in his name. Refer to next chapter for further elaboration upon this.

others rejected it due to envy because the anticipated Prophet was not from their race or tribe. Pride and arrogance came in their way. In the case of others, the desire to hold on to wealth hindered them. Others desired to maintain their high status in society and resented that Islām made no distinction in terms of race or class. And yet others were unable to leave the way of their forefathers who had erred and strayed from prior revelation. The previous Prophets and Messengers such as Abraham, Moses, Solomon, David, Jesus and John (عَلَيْهِمُ السَّلَامُ) are from the brethren of Muḥammad (ﷺ) in the faith of Islām (submission to one God alone). Whoever rejected Muḥammad (ﷺ) has automatically rejected all previous messengers because making distinctions between them by believing in some and rejecting others is not permissible in any revealed Book.[49]

The Prophet Muḥammad (ﷺ) was described by his Companions as being the most handsome of people in appearance, the best of them in manners, neither exceedingly tall nor exceedingly short and in his complexion he was neither very white, nor very dark nor brown, but illuminous.[50] He was of medium build with broad shoulders and his hair was neither too straight nor too curly and it would curl to his

[49] Learned Torah Jews know that Islām was the religion of all the Israelite Prophets and the name of "Allāh" and His religion, "Islām" is equivalent in the languages of Hebrew, Arabic and Aramaic (Syriac). Whoever rejected Muḥammad (ﷺ) from those given scripture from the previous nations after their knowledge that he is a Messenger has automatically rejected the previous Messengers. This is because it is not permitted to make any distinction between the Messengers of Allāh. They were brethren in faith and were sent by the same Lord and with the same message. Allāh (عَزَّوَجَلَّ) stated, **"The Messenger has believed in what was revealed to him from his Lord, and [so have] the believers. All of them have believed in Allāh and His angels and His books and His messengers, [saying], 'We make no distinction between any of His messengers.' And they say, 'We hear and we obey. [We seek] Your forgiveness, our Lord, and to You is the [final] destination'."** (2:285) and **"But they who believe in Allāh and His messengers and do not discriminate between any of them - to those He is going to give their rewards. And ever is Allāh Forgiving and Merciful."** (4:152).

[50] Related by al-Bukhārī (no. 3549).

earlobes or reach his shoulders. When he smiled, his face radiated as if it was a piece of the moon.[51] His truthfulness and trustworthiness was known and famous with the tribe of Quraysh who knew him as al-Ṣādiq (the truthful) and al-Amīn (the trustworthy). Anas bin Mālik (رَضِيَ اللَّهُ عَنْهُ) who served the Prophet (ﷺ) for ten years said that he had not touched silk or velvet smoother than the palm of the Prophet's hand and nor a fragrance more pleasant than his fragrance[52] and he also said in those ten years, the Prophet (ﷺ) never scolded him once and never once said 'Why did you do this?' or 'Why did you not do this?' Anas also said that the Prophet was the best of people in manners. He also mentioned the excessive generosity of the Prophet (ﷺ). He was gentle and forbearing, never used crude or foul language, and would always take the easier and least burdensome of two options, never placing burdens and hardships upon anyone. Abu Saʾīd al-Khudrī (رَضِيَ اللَّهُ عَنْهُ) mentioned that the Prophet (ﷺ) was extremely modest and shy, more so than a bashful virgin.[53] He was the bravest of people, was deeply pious and displayed awe of his Lord, placing his utmost trust in Allāh.

He commanded people - as did all the Prophets before him - to shun the worship of idols, statues, stones, trees, the elements, the forces, prophets, angels, jinn, the righteous, whether living or dead. Thereafter, he commanded benevolence to parents, lowering the wing of humility to them, kindness to the orphan and widow and frequent giving of charity. He was the most merciful and kind of people to his family and dependents and would say, "*Allāh will not be merciful to the one who is not merciful to the people.*"[54] He declared cleanliness to be one half of faith and purity of the heart to be the foundation of outward deeds. He forbade lying, breaking of covenants, and treachery. He also

---

[51] Related by al-Bukhārī (no. 3556).

[52] Related by al-Bukhārī (no. 3561).

[53] This trait may be hard to fathom in some societies where the notion of modesty, purity, chastity and virginity hold no value and may even be considered blameworthy qualities, if not *dirty qualities.*

[54] Related by al-Bukhārī and Muslim.

forbade usury, intoxicants, gambling, murder, killing innocents, embezzling wealth and falsely accusing chaste women.

Despite thirteen years of sustained abuse, mockery, physical harm and the torture and killing of his companions, he never initiated violence and was prohibited to do so. Forced to leave Makkah because of rising hostility and repeated assassination attempts, he endured another ten years of schemes, intrigues and war against him and his companions. He was commanded in the Qur'ān to be patient and to endure harm. Allāh (عَزَّوَجَلَّ) stated, "**O Prophet, indeed We have sent you as a witness and a bringer of good tidings and a warner and as one who invites to Allāh , by His permission, and as an illuminating lamp. And give good tidings to the believers that they will have from Allāh great bounty. And do not obey the disbelievers and the hypocrites but do not harm them, and rely upon Allāh. And sufficient is Allāh as Disposer of affairs.**" (33:45-48).[55] Only after exhausting the avenues of peaceful resolution through mutual understandings, truces and treaties, he was first granted permission and then obligated to defend himself against his enemies. And when they proved to be treacherous and did not honour their treaties and covenants he was commanded to pursue them to put an end to their mischief and tribulation on the land. At the end of his call, he marched into Makkah in total peace (not war), victorious, having shown mercy and compassion to his enemies and having granted them free passage. Many of them were left dumbfounded and awestruck at the kindness, clemency and grandeur of Muḥammad (ﷺ) and hastily accepted Islām. This is engraved in history. This is the noble Prophet of Islām and his lofty character. Cartoons do not and will not rewrite history.

[55] The earliest exegetes such as Ibn 'Abbās (رَضِيَٱللَّهُعَنْهُ) and Qatādah (رَحِمَهُٱللَّهُ), said, in explanation of this verse, "[Meaning], have patience upon their harm" as is cited from them by al-Baghawī in his exegesis. The Salafī scholar of the 20th century, Shaykh 'Abd al-Raḥmān bin Nāsir al-Sa'dī commented on this verse, "Do not obey them in every affair that hinders from the path of Allāh but this does not require that they be harmed." Refer to *Taysīr al-Karīm al-Raḥmān*. And the famous commentator, Ibn Kathīr, said, "Meaning, pardon and overlook them and entrust the affair to Allāh." *Tafsīr al-Qur'ān al-Aẓīm*.

Muḥammad (صَلَّى ٱللَّهُ عَلَيْهِ وَسَلَّمَ): An Exalted Remembrance

Allāh (عَزَّوَجَلَّ) stated in what He revealed to Muḥammad (صَلَّى ٱللَّهُ عَلَيْهِ وَسَلَّمَ):

وَرَفَعْنَا لَكَ ذِكْرَكَ

And we have raised high your mention. (94:4)

There are over one and a half billion Muslims on the Earth, spanning across all continents and all ethnicities and races. Five times a day, the name of Muḥammad (صَلَّى ٱللَّهُ عَلَيْهِ وَسَلَّمَ) is mentioned in the call to prayer alongside that of Allāh, the Lord of the Worlds, the same Lord of Abraham, Moses, Solomon, David, Jesus and John (عَلَيْهِمُ ٱلسَّلَامُ). In every prayer, a Muslim makes mention of Muḥammad (صَلَّى ٱللَّهُ عَلَيْهِ وَسَلَّمَ), asking for peace, mercy and blessings to be showered upon him. Every time his name is mentioned, a Muslims says, "M*ay peace and blessings be upon him.*" His name is **the most popular** name on the planet. Every day, he is **the most remembered** person on the planet. Of the closest of all the people to Muḥammad (صَلَّى ٱللَّهُ عَلَيْهِ وَسَلَّمَ) from those who traversed the Earth is Jesus (عَلَيْهِ ٱلسَّلَامُ) - he who came to be through a spoken Word and a Spirit sent from Allāh. The Prophet Muḥammad (صَلَّى ٱللَّهُ عَلَيْهِ وَسَلَّمَ) said, "*Both in this world and the next, I am the nearest of all the people to the son of Mary, and all the Prophets are paternal brothers, and there has been no prophet between me and him (Jesus).*"[56]

But Muḥammad (صَلَّى ٱللَّهُ عَلَيْهِ وَسَلَّمَ) is remembered and revered as a Prophet, not a deity.[57] He strictly prohibited physical representations and

[56] Reported by Imām al-Bukhāri in his Ṣaḥīḥ.

[57] Jesus did not command his followers to worship him but he commanded them to worship his Lord and their Lord. The message of Muḥammad (صَلَّى ٱللَّهُ عَلَيْهِ وَسَلَّمَ) is the actual message of Jesus and of all previous Prophets. In the Qur'ān, the Lord of Jesus says, **"And remember when Allāh will say (on the Day of Resurrection): 'O Jesus, son of Mary! Did you say unto men: 'Worship me and my mother as two gods besides Allāh?' He will say: 'Glory be to You! It was not for me to say what I had no right to say. Had I said such a thing,**

idolization as this is the starting point and from the ways and means of erecting and worshipping false deities.[58] He prohibited excessive praise of himself above and beyond his status as a humble slave and messenger of Allāh and warned Muslims not to follow the path taken by Christians towards Jesus (عَلَيْهِ ٱلسَّلَامُ). He strictly prohibited people from bowing and prostrating to him. He disliked people standing up for him. He ordered his companions not to imitate the nations who stand for their kings and leaders. When an outsider would come to see the Prophet (صَلَّى ٱللَّٰهُ عَلَيْهِ وَسَلَّمَ), he would not be able distinguish him from his

---

You would surely have known it. You know what is in my inner-self though I do not know what is in Yours, truly, You, only You are the All-Knower of all that is hidden and unseen. Never did I say to them aught except what You (Allāh) did command me to say: 'Worship Allāh, my Lord and your Lord.' And I was a witness over them while I dwelt amongst them, but when You took me up, You were the Watcher over them, and You are a Witness to all things. If You punish them, they are Your slaves, and if You forgive them, verily, You, only You are the All-Mighty, the All-Wise'." (5:116-118). When Christ's message was received by the pagans of Rome and the Mediterranean, the mythology of those civilizations was weaved and incorporated into the message, thereby altering and perverting the original. Concepts of *trinity, begotten son, sun-god, resurrection, rebirth* and *redeemer* were widespread during that era with respect to the dieties of the Egyptians, Greeks, Persians, and Romans such as *Osiris, Horus, Isis, Mithra, Dionysus, Attis, Bāl*. Constantine, the pagan Roman emperor, blended Christianity with elements of paganism and made it the state religion. His primary motivation was to consolidate political power by uniting both Christian and pagan worshippers in his kingdom upon a new faith. It became more or less impossible for any Christian to know and practice the true way of Jesus a couple of centuries after him. The only way Christians today can follow the message of Jesus is by following the final Messenger, Muḥammad (صَلَّى ٱللَّٰهُ عَلَيْهِ وَسَلَّمَ) who was sent with a perfection of the Islām brought by previous Prophets and Messengers.

[58] **The Prohibition of Depicting the Prophets**. The prohibition of depicting the Prophet Muḥammad (صَلَّى ٱللَّٰهُ عَلَيْهِ وَسَلَّمَ) falls within the generalized prohibition of physical representations, pictures and their likes of living things which is a matter of consensus amongst orthodox Muslim scholars. The fact that the depiction of the Prophet (صَلَّى ٱللَّٰهُ عَلَيْهِ وَسَلَّمَ) can be found in later Islāmic history does not make the action lawful *from a legislative point of view*. The lawful (*ḥalāl*) and unlawful (*ḥarām*) are known through the texts of the Qur'ān and the authentic Prophetic traditions and not the actions of Muslims.

companions in clothing and appearance. He was humbler than any king who ever walked the Earth yet respected in a manner that no king has ever been respected. He aided in household chores, relieved others of difficulty and showed respect to the old and mercy to the young. Frequently, he visited the weak, the sick and the poor and would mend his own clothes and shoes. It is legislated for Muslims to mention and supplicate for the Prophet (صَلَّى ٱللَّٰهُ عَلَيْهِ وَسَلَّمَ) during their activities throughout the day, including but not limited to: Within the call to prayer, after the call to prayer, when performing the funeral prayer for the deceased, when giving sermons, when supplicating to Allāh in general, when entering and leaving the mosque, when writing or mentioning his name and so on.[59] Pencil cartoons do not and will not rewrite history and nor will they diminish or lower the exalted rank of Muḥammad (صَلَّى ٱللَّٰهُ عَلَيْهِ وَسَلَّمَ). Indeed, the truth has been preserved on the tongue of unbiased, objective, fair-minded non-Muslims. **David George Hogarth** (d. 1927), English archaeologist author and keeper of the Ashmolean Museum, Oxford, wrote, "Serious or trivial, his daily behaviour has instituted a canon which millions observe this day with conscious mimicry. No one regarded by any section of the human race as Perfect Man has been imitated so minutely. The conduct of the Founder of Christianity has not so governed the ordinary life of his followers. Moreover, no Founder of a religion has been left on **so solitary an eminence** as the Muslim Apostle."[60] The pencil of the immoral cartoonist is no match for the testimony of the cultivated, refined, intellectual, mannerly gentleman. The barking of the dog harms neither the clouds nor the peaks of mountains.

[59] Refer to *Ḥuqūq al-Nabiyy wal-Intiṣār li Sharīʿatihī* of Shaykh Rabīʿ bin Hādī (Dār al-Mīrāth, 2010) p. 42. Refer also to the excellent book by the Salafī Scholar, Ibn al-Qayyim, "*Jalā al-Afhām Fī Faḍl al-Ṣalāt wal-Salām ʿalā Muḥammad Khayr al-Anām.*" In the third chapter of this book, Ibn al-Qayyim outlines forty-one (41) situations in which it is legislated either by obligation or commendation for a person to supplicate for the Messenger of Allāh (صَلَّى ٱللَّٰهُ عَلَيْهِ وَسَلَّمَ) with peace, blessings and honourable mention.

[60] In his book, *Arabia*, Oxford, 1922, p. 52

Muḥammad (صَلَّى ٱللَّٰهُ عَلَيْهِ وَسَلَّمَ): A Mercy To The Worlds

Muḥammad (صَلَّى ٱللَّٰهُ عَلَيْهِ وَسَلَّمَ) is the most upright, complete and perfect of characters and he is the model of upright conduct for every person desiring perfection in character. The exemplification of this in his conduct and behaviour in every field of life has been documented and fills volume upon volume, generation after generation, century after century until this day of ours. He is the most written-about man in history. Whether you like it or not, one day or another, you will be forced to go beyond the hype, commotion and propaganda and make an objective, unbiased study of this lofty man. Since, it is impossible to cover his virtues in a thick volume, let alone a work of this size, we can only but give three illustrations of the mercy in his call, his teachings and the commandments which he conveyed from Allāh, his Lord and the Lord of Abraham, Moses and Jesus (عَلَيْهِمُ ٱلسَّلَامُ). The first example illustrates his patience, forgiveness and mercy.

LESSONS FROM THE INCIDENT AT ṬĀ'IF

When the Prophet Muḥammad (صَلَّى ٱللَّٰهُ عَلَيْهِ وَسَلَّمَ) saw the hostility and resistance of the polytheists of Quraysh to his message and despaired of its acceptance he thought about going to places outside of Makkah in the hope that his message would be received more favourably. He chose Ṭā'if because it was the next most prominent city after Makkāh. Further, it was inhabited by the powerful tribe of Thaqīf and was not a great distance from Makkah, a journey of fifty or so miles. He walked on his two feet without a riding animal until they became swollen and painful. When he entered the city, he invited the leaders of Thaqīf to the religion of Islām which called to pure monotheism, equality of standing before Allāh between the slave and the chief, the white and the black, the brown and the red and to the prohibition of usury. Due to their knowledge that Islām was not beneficial to their worldly interests and their monopoly over the people, they rejected Islām but in no ordinary way. They were extremely stern and harsh in their rejection despite the Prophet's gentleness and kindness to them in his call. In fact, they rejected his message with biting mockery and derision. The Prophet (ﷺ) remained in Ṭā'if for around ten days inviting them to Islām with gentleness and benevolence. However, the leaders of Thaqīf displayed the complete absence of basic manners known to the Arabs of honouring the guest and incited their children to throw stones and rocks at the Prophet in order to drive him out of the city. This caused him to bleed as he made attempts to flee from this persecution, almost passing out whilst crawling. Within this state he supplicated and complained of his own weakness and deficiency to his Lord in not having met with success at Ṭā'if. His wife, 'Ā'ishah (رَضِيَ اللَّهُ عَنْهَا) would later ask him, "O Messenger of Allāh, was there a day that came upon you more severe than the day of Uḥud?" The Prophet (ﷺ) recounted the rejection he met and explained whilst he was returning from Tā'if Jibrīl (Gabriel) appeared to him and said, "Allāh has heard what your people have been saying to you and how they responded to you. Allāh has sent the angel of the mountains so that you can command him to do as you wish." Then the angel of the mountain called him and after greeting him, said, "O Muḥammad, order whatever you wish. If you like, I will cause the two mountains to fall upon them." The Prophet (ﷺ) replied, "*No, for I hope that Allāh will bring forth from their progeny people who will worship Allāh alone and not associate any partners with him.*"[61]

On other occasions of meeting harm, the Prophet (ﷺ) would say, "*May Allāh have mercy upon Moses, for he was harmed much more than this and showed patience.*"[62] And he (ﷺ) also informed about a Prophet amongst the Prophets whose people beat him and he began to say, "*O Allāh, forgive my people for they do not know*"[63] and he himself would say the likes of this when met with harm.[64] Thus, the Prophet combined

---

[61] The report of 'Ā'ishah his related by al-Bukhārī.

[62] Related by al-Bukhārī (no. 3510) and Muslim (no. 1062).

[63] Related by al-Bukhārī (no. 3477) and Muslim (no. 1792).

[64] Related by al-Ṭabarānī in *al-Kabīr* (no. 5862) with a connected chain whose narrators are trustworthy except Zahrah bin 'Umar al-Ḍabbī al-Taymī who is mentioned by al-Bukhārī in *al-Tarīkh al-Kabīr* (3/443), Ibn Abī Ḥātim in *al-Jarḥ*

between three affairs: Pardoning those who harmed him, seeking forgiveness for them and excusing them because they did not know. This tradition demonstrates the degree of compassion and mercy possessed by the Prophet (ﷺ). He was never, ever motivated by revenge for worldly or personal reasons, but he was eagerly desirous of guiding people and saving them from punishment in the Hereafter. The second example is an illustration of his clemency and mercy towards a person who set out to assassinate him.

THE STORY OF THE ASSASSIN THUMĀMAH BIN ĀTHĀL

As the days and years passed, many people began to enter into Islām. One day a person would be a staunch, avowed enemy and the next day he would be humbled into submission by the sheer force, simplicity, purity and power of the message that struck and captured his heart. Prior to accepting Islām, numerous people tried to murder the Prophet (ﷺ). There is the example of Thumāmah bin Athāl.[65] He was a chief of the Banū Ḥanīfah tribe and a king amongst the kings of the region of al-Yamāmah. He was obeyed and listened to by his people. The Prophet (ﷺ) would send letters out to the chiefs and leaders to invite them to Islām. When Thumāmāh received one such letter, he was taken by his pride and honour. He even killed a number of Muslims due to his hatred and outrage. After some time Thumāmah desired to perform ʿumrah[66] and as he was passing by al-Madīnah he was captured by a group of Muslims who did not know his identity. They brought him into the city, tied him to one of the pillars in the mosque and waited for the Prophet (ﷺ) to determine his affair.

---

wal-Taʿdīl (3/615) and both of them did not mention him with either disparagement or praise and Ibn Ḥibbān mentioned him in *al-Thiqāt* (6/344).

[65] The story can be founded the collections of Prophetic tradition such as al-Bukhārī, Muslim, Abū Dāwūd and the various biographical accounts such as *Sīrah Ibn Hishām*.

[66] The lesser pilgrimage. The polytheists used to perform the rituals of Ḥajj prior to Islām but upon their particular way which included invoking and worshipping other deities alongside Allāh.

When the Prophet came and saw the face of the captive, he said to the Companions, "Do you know whom you have captured?" They replied in the negative and he said, "This is Thumāmah bin Athāl al-Ḥanafī so be benevolent to him." When the Prophet returned some time later he ordered the Companions to gather food for Thumāmah. He also commanded a camel to be milked for Thumāmāh to drink from. All of this took place before the Prophet (ﷺ) spoke even a word to him.

Then the Prophet came to Thumāmah and said to him, "What [purpose] have you have come with O Thumāmah?" Thumāmah said, "O Muḥammad I have come with goodness. If you take my blood, you will have killed a man who has already taken blood. If you set me free you will be doing favour to someone who will be grateful. If you seek wealth, then ask and you will be granted [any amount]." Thumāmah was prepared to meet his fate with honour and dignity. The Prophet left him and returned to him the next day, asking the very same question. Thumāmah gave the very same answer. During this time, Thumāmah was being honoured and treated well. Whilst tied to the pillar in the mosque he was observing the Muslims and their worship. The next day the Prophet (ﷺ) came to him again and asked the same question to which Thumāmah replied with the same answer as before, "O Muḥammad I have come with goodness. If you take my blood, you will have killed a man who has already taken blood. If you set me free you will be doing favour to someone who will be grateful. If you seek wealth, then ask and you will be granted [any amount]." The Prophet (ﷺ) ordered that he be released.

When Thumāmah reached the outskirts of the city and had time to reflect on his experience, he stopped by a garden to think further. He then bathed with the water in the garden, returned to the mosque and announced, "I bear witness that there is no deity worthy of worship [in truth] except Allāh alone and I bear witness that Muḥammad is Allāh's Messenger." Thumāmah continued, addressing the Prophet (ﷺ), "By Allāh O Muḥammad, there was no face on the Earth which I disliked more than yours but now your face has become the most beloved face to me. By Allāh there was no path I disliked more than yours, but now it is the most beloved to me. By Allāh there was no town I disliked more than your town, but now it is the most beloved to me." Thumāmah then said, "I killed some of your followers earlier, what should I pay for that crime?" The Prophet replied, "*There is nothing upon you for that O Thumāmah, for Islām wipes out everything that was before it.*"

He then asked for permission to proceed to perform the ʿumrah and the Prophet (ﷺ) taught him the correct way to perform it, upon pure monotheism. Thumāmah entered the city of Makkah whilst making the Islāmic call for the pilgrimage out aloud. He invoked only Allāh, the creator of the Heavens and Earth, and shunned the mention of other deities. The polytheists were disturbed at hearing this call and drew out their swords to kill the audacious person who dared to proclaim such a call in their midst. When they recognized it was Thumāmah, they stopped out of fear of the consequences from his people. The food supply to Makkah was largely from al-Yamāmah and they feared that it would be cut off. Thumāmah performed the ʿumrah and returned without harm. Thereafter, he resolved to harm the Quraysh just as they had harmed and waged war against the Prophet (ﷺ) and the Muslims. He cut ties with them and also informed them that not a single grain of wheat will come to them from al-Yamāmah. Feeling the effect, the polytheists of Quraysh complained to Prophet Muḥammad (ﷺ) about Thumāmah through a messenger. They said, "He claims ties of kinship should be respected, yet has cut off from the Quraysh. He has killed fathers with swords and is now killing children with starvation."

The Quraysh said this with their full knowledge that years earlier, they had starved the Prophet and his followers in Makkāh for three full years by imposing economic and social sanctions upon them through a boycott of Banū Hāshim.[67] This had harmed the Muslims a great deal and was a severe trial for them. But the Prophet (صَلَّىٱللَّهُعَلَيْهِوَسَلَّمَ) wrote to Thumāmah to lift the boycott and to resume the food supplies to the residents of Makkah.[68] There are some great lessons in this story[69] for both the hateful, spiteful, ignorant Islamophobe and the savage Khārijite terrorist. Muḥammad (صَلَّىٱللَّهُعَلَيْهِوَسَلَّمَ) was not sent with the goal of killing people and dispossessing them of their land and wealth. Rather, he was sent with the goal of guiding them and taking them out of darkness into light. His astounding degree of patience towards the harm that came to him and his astounding degree of clemency and mercy towards his enemies despite having the ability to harm them in many instances is a sign and a lesson for people of reflection - both Muslims and non-Muslims. The third example is an illustration of the mercy and kindness in the teachings he conveyed.

THE RIGHTS OF THE NON-MUSLIM NEIGHBOUR

Allāh (عَزَّوَجَلَّ) stated in what He revealed to Muḥammad (صَلَّىٱللَّهُعَلَيْهِوَسَلَّمَ):

وَمَآ أَرۡسَلۡنَٰكَ إِلَّا رَحۡمَةٗ لِّلۡعَٰلَمِينَ

And we have not sent you except as

[67] The leading clans of Quraysh entered into an alliance to boycott the Banū Hāshim and Banū Muṭṭālib economically and socially. Both trade and inter-marriage were prohibited. The Banū Hāshim were a commercial rival to those clans and they had been giving protection to Muḥammad (صَلَّىٱللَّهُعَلَيْهِوَسَلَّمَ) on purely tribal grounds. Hence, both non-Muslims and Muslims were boycotted during this three year period. The situation got so dire that the Muslims had to eat the leaves of trees and crying children could be heard in the valleys to which they had been forced to retreat. Eventually, the boycott collapsed and failed to break the resolve of the Muslims.

[68] Compare this to the well-researched and documented actions of European leaders, kings and queens in the colonial era of deliberately implementing economic and trade policies to exacerbate the effects of famines as a means of culling colonized populations by the millions as a means of tightening their grip on lands and resources for self-enrichment.

[69] There are hundreds of such lessons in the Prophetic biography.

a mercy to the worlds. (21:107)

From the abundant manifestations of the merciful teachings of the Prophet (صَلَّى ٱللَّهُ عَلَيْهِ وَسَلَّمَ) is the right of the neighbour. After the rights of parents and blood-relatives, it is the greatest of rights and applies to every neighbour, Muslim or non-Muslim.

The Prophet Muḥammad (صَلَّى ٱللَّهُ عَلَيْهِ وَسَلَّمَ) was commanded to emphatically stress this right. He said, "*The [angel] Jibrīl (Gabriel) has not ceased advising me with respect to the neighbour until I thought he (the neigbour) would be made to inherit (from his fellow neighbour).*"[70] The Prophet also negated complete faith from the one who does not withhold from harming his neighbour, "*By Allāh, he does not have faith, by Allāh, he does not have faith, by Allāh, he does not have faith whose neighbour is not safe from his harm.*"[71] And in another authentic tradition, he said, "*Whoever believes in Allāh and the Final Day (of Reckoning), let him honour his neighbour.*"[72] Under the chapter heading, "*The Jewish Neighbour*," the famous collector of Prophetic traditions, Imām al-Bukhārī relates the following authentic tradition from the commentator of the Qurʾān, Mujāhid (d. 102H), who said: "I was with ʿAbdullāh bin ʿAmr (a companion of the Prophet) whilst his servant was preparing a sheep (for a meal) and he said, 'O servant! When you have finished (cooking the meal) then begin by offering to our Jewish neighbour (first).' So a man present said, "The Jew, may Allāh rectify you?' He replied, 'I heard the Prophet (صَلَّى ٱللَّهُ عَلَيْهِ وَسَلَّمَ) advising with (kindness) to the neighbour (with such emphasis) until we feared he would relate to us (through revelation) that the (neighbour) is to inherit (from his fellow neighbour)'."[73] The neighbour in Islām is defined as the one who lives in the vicinity of any direction, left, right, front, back and would also include above and below in flats and apartments.

---

[70] Reported by Muslim in his Ṣaḥīḥ.

[71] Related by al-Bukhārī in Kitāb al-Adab.

[72] Related by al-Bukhārī and Muslim.

[73] Related by al-Bukhārī in *al-Adab al-Mufrad.*

For that reason, if as a non-Muslim, you have a Muslim neighbour and you have not received benevolent treatment, the cooking of a meal, a visit when sick, a gift, household assistance or what customarily enters into kindness then he or she is neglecting a part of your right. And if you are not secure from his or her harm, then know that this is a sinful Muslim who is in violation of one of the greatest of rights whose fulfilment has been made obligatory upon every single Muslim. One should not be deceived by the outward piety or devotion displayed by such a person while he or she is neglectful of this duty which is evidence for the genuineness of a person's faith. Abu Hurayrah (رَضِيَٱللَّهُعَنْهُ) reports that a man mentioned to the Prophet (ﷺ) that a particular woman is mentioned with plentiful prayer, charity and fasting but she abuses her neighbour with her tongue. The Prophet said, "*She is in the Hellfire.*" Then the man said that a particular woman is mentioned with little prayer, fasting and charity, but she gives the cheese of oxen in charity and does not harm her neighbour. The Prophet said, "*She is in Paradise.*"[74]

These are the teachings of the Prophet Muḥammad (ﷺ). Neither terrorists nor cartoonists are able to misrepresent the teachings of this lofty and noble Prophet because his teachings are preserved through the highest standards of oral transmission ever known in the history of mankind. The Muslim nation was given the isnād (the chain of narration)[75] and the rigorous science associated with it that is unparallelled and unmatched in history.

---

[74] Related by al-Bukhārī in *al-Adab al-Mufrad*, al-Bayḥaqī and others and it is declared ṣaḥīḥ by al-Albānī in *Ṣaḥīḥ al-Targhīb wal-Tarhīb* and he also mentions it in *Ṣaḥīḥ al-Adab al-Mufrad* and *al-Silsilah al-Ṣaḥīḥah*.

[75] The word *isnād* means *ascription* and refers to the chain of authorities through whom the Prophetic traditions were transmitted and collected. It is a complex, highly-developed, rigorous science. No nation prior to the Islāmic nation was given such a science to aid in the preservation of revealed knowledge. Without preservation of the Prophetic traditions, explanation of the Qur'ān and extraction of legal rulings would not be possible and the religion would have been distorted and wasted. ʿAbdullāh bin al-Mubārak (d. 181H, 8th century CE) said, "The *isnād* is from the religion, had it not been for

The science of *ḥadīth* (Prophetic traditions) allows certainty to be attained in the veracity of knowledge transmitted from the Prophet (صَلَّىٰٱللَّهُعَلَيْهِوَسَلَّمَ). Through it, lies, fabrications, erroneous claims and baseless reports are separated from the authentic reports. Further, just as the texts are preserved through this science, their meanings and correct contextual interpretations are also preserved through the Prophet's Companions (رَضِيَٱللَّهُعَنْهُمْ) and in turn through the trustworthy scholars in every generation. The Prophet Muḥammad (صَلَّىٰٱللَّهُعَلَيْهِوَسَلَّمَ) said, "*This knowledge will be carried by the trustworthy ones of every generation. They will remove from it the distortion of those going beyond bounds, the fabrications of falsifiers and the false-interpretations of the ignorant.*"[76] Thus the orthodox Sunnī Muslims are able to repel, in a rigorous, scientific manner, every saying falsely ascribed to the Prophet (صَلَّىٰٱللَّهُعَلَيْهِوَسَلَّمَ), every false interpretation of an authentic text and every attempted distortion of the teachings of Islām. Because prior messages were not intended as universal guidance for all mankind, their preservation was not specified unlike that of the Qur'ān and the Prophetic traditions. It is not possible for anyone to attempt to misrepresent any issue without some or all of the scholars of the Muslims being able to expose his lie in a rigorous scientific manner.

---

the *isnād*, anyone could have said what he willed." Related by the famous Imām Muslim bin al-Ḥajjāj in his introduction to his collection of Prophetic traditions. European Orientalists who began to study Islām over the past few centuries have tried to undermine this system as part of a broader objective to weaken Islāmic sciences. However their ignorance of the sophistication and depth of this science, studying it as unqualified outsiders interested only in undermining the science and not understanding it objectively, left them in a hapless state with glaring contradictions in their theories and claims. A large body of literature exists comprising a robust, powerful response by competent Muslim authorities in this regard.

[76] *Mishkāt al-Maṣābīh* with checking of Shaykh al-Albānī (1/53).

Muslims Are Prohibited to Mock Other Deities

Allāh (عَزَّوَجَلَّ) stated in what He revealed to Muḥammad (صَلَّى ٱللَّهُ عَلَيْهِ وَسَلَّمَ):

وَلَا تَسُبُّوا۟ ٱلَّذِينَ يَدْعُونَ مِن دُونِ ٱللَّهِ فَيَسُبُّوا۟ ٱللَّهَ عَدْوًۢا بِغَيْرِ عِلْمٍ ۗ كَذَٰلِكَ زَيَّنَّا لِكُلِّ أُمَّةٍ عَمَلَهُمْ ثُمَّ إِلَىٰ رَبِّهِم مَّرْجِعُهُمْ فَيُنَبِّئُهُم بِمَا كَانُوا۟ يَعْمَلُونَ ﴿١٠٨﴾

And insult not those whom they worship besides Allāh, lest they insult Allāh wrongfully without knowledge. Thus We have made fair-seeming to each people its own doings; then to their Lord is their return and He shall then inform them of all that they used to do. (6:108).

Even though Muslims reject the worship of deities besides the deity in truth of Abraham, Moses, Jesus and Muhammad (صَلَّى ٱللَّهُ عَلَيْهِ وَسَلَّمَ) and may disagree with and criticize the rationale, if there is any, behind the worship of stones, trees, the elements, the forces, animals, prophets or the righteous or any created entities, they are prohibited from abusing, reviling and mocking the deities of others even though upon the alleged foundation of *absolute* freedom of speech they would be at liberty to do so.

The late Salafi Scholar of the 20th century, ʿAbd al-Raḥmān bin Nāsir al-Saʿdī (رَحِمَهُ ٱللَّهُ) said in his commentary on the above verse: "Allāh forbade the revilement of the deities of the polytheists because they are (naturally) protective of their religion and are strongly partisan towards it and because the deed of every nation has been made fair-seeming to it. Hence they see it as something good and defend it through every means until they would even revile Allāh, the Lord of the Worlds [out of zeal and defence of their deities]."[77]

[77] Refer to *Taysīr al-Karīm al-Raḥmān Fī Tafsir Kalām al-Mannān.*

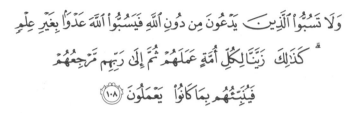

Thus, Muslims are prohibited to revile, mock and abuse the deities of others because it would lead to escalation and violation of sanctities. Orthodox Muslims who follow the Prophetic traditions boast of this legislation and all the wisdoms surrounding it. They venerate this legislation by withholding from mocking the deities of others and what they consider to be sacred, let alone withholding from engaging in violence which the Islāmic legislation has outlawed. Muslims are proud of this legislation because it demonstrates the forbearance enjoined upon them - even in matters that are sacred to them. Indeed, when the polytheists mocked, ridiculed and abused the Prophet (صَلَّى ٱللَّٰهُ عَلَيْهِ وَسَلَّمَ), he was commanded in the Qur'ān:

وَٱصْبِرْ عَلَىٰ مَا يَقُولُونَ وَٱهْجُرْهُمْ هَجْرًا جَمِيلًا

And be patient over what they say and avoid them with gracious avoidance. (73:10)

A Muslim's strict adherence to this injunction should never be affected by the spiteful pencil of the cartoonist because unlike the cartoonist and the savage terrorist, Islām teaches its adherents to be honourable and dignified in the face of abuse. Those who come out on the streets, driven by uncontrolled rage, and do that which Islām has prohibited of demonstrating and rioting and what they often lead to of the destruction of wealth, property and even life, then they are not followers of the Prophet (صَلَّى ٱللَّٰهُ عَلَيْهِ وَسَلَّمَ) in this behaviour. Rather, they are weak souls, ignorant and deficient in faith, overtaken by emotions and subject to being exploited to their own detriment and to the detriment of Islām. Likewise, those who take innocent lives and terrorize societies, they are not followers of the Prophet (صَلَّى ٱللَّٰهُ عَلَيْهِ وَسَلَّمَ) in this behaviour. Loving and respecting the Prophet (صَلَّى ٱللَّٰهُ عَلَيْهِ وَسَلَّمَ) is by adorning oneself with the beautiful character he possessed and from its greatest qualities is forbearance, patience and maintaining dignity and honour in the face of abuse and placing one's reliance upon Allāh (عَزَّ وَجَلَّ), the best disposer of affairs. This is what we see throughout the entire biography of the Prophet (صَلَّى ٱللَّٰهُ عَلَيْهِ وَسَلَّمَ).

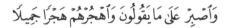

Muslims Are Prohibited From Lying to Make Others Laugh

Just as Muslims are proud of the legislation that prohibits them from mocking the deities of others in order to prevent escalation and violation of sanctities, they are also proud that they are prohibited from telling lies in order to make people laugh - which is the way of the comedians, cartoonists and others whose profession is founded upon lying - the most dishonourable of ways to make a living.[78] The Prophet (ﷺ), exalted in his standard of character, said:

ويل للذي يحدث بالحديث ليضحك به القوم فيكذب ويل له ويل له

Which means, "*Woe be to the one who relates a story in order to make people laugh but lies therein, woe be to him and woe be to him.*"[79] On the basis of this tradition, it is unlawful for a Muslim who follows the Prophet of Islām to tell lies just to make people laugh. The companion of the Prophet, ʿAbdullāh bin Masʿūd (رضي الله عنه) said, "*Lying, whether seriously or in jest is not befitting.*" The commentators upon the Prophetic traditions explain the level of honesty a Muslim is to maintain in light of this Prophetic teaching. The commentator, Muḥammad Shams al-Dīn Al-Aẓīmabādī, says, "In this tradition there is an indication that what some of the people speak with when the child cries for example - of words made in jest [to console the child] or telling a lie about giving the child something or to make the child fear [so that the child stops crying] - that this enters into the lying which is prohibited in this tradition."[80] The Muslim who follows this Prophet of lofty, impeccable character and noble manners does not tell lies,

[78] As for humour based upon statements which are true, Prophet Muḥammad (ﷺ) engaged in this and allowed it so long as it is done in moderation and does not entail backbiting or mockery of others. Protection of peoples' honour is amongst the greatest objectives of the Islāmic Sharīʿah.

[79] Related by Aḥmad, Abū Dāwūd, al-Tirmidhī and numerous other authorities.

[80] In *ʿAwn al-Maʿbūd* (13/235).

neither in jest nor in seriousness, nor to make people laugh, nor in sarcasm or mockery and not even with children. Muslims boast of this legislation. They are proud of this legislation. This legislation is the moral club hammer which smashes the fraudulent pencil of the cartoonist who tells lies and invents fabrications in jest to grant relief to the baser instincts of his soul in the name of *freedom of expression.* Just as it smashes the way of the terrorist in resorting to lies and treachery in order to cause destruction in both religious and worldly affairs. The terrorist, in perpetrating his evil actions, has to operate through lies, deception and treachery in relation to his contractual obligations and covenants in the society he has chosen to live. Thus, when Islām demands such a standard of uprightness and honesty in that it prohibits lying even in jest, then it shows the degree to which the dishonesty and treachery of the terrorist's actions are condemned by Islām. This is what the Prophet of Islām (صَلَّى ٱللَّهُ عَلَيْهِ وَسَلَّمَ) taught Muslims and it illustrates that Islām has come with the perfection of character. This is why the Prophet (صَلَّى ٱللَّهُ عَلَيْهِ وَسَلَّمَ) said, "*Indeed I have (only) been sent that I may perfect the noblest of manners.*"[81] From the greatest foundations of perfect character is being truthful and not telling lies. As for the claimed *right to offend*, if a person becomes offended as a result of something truthful being said, that is one thing.[82] But as for when it is based upon lies, misrepresentations and outright falsehood, it becomes malicious intent and no longer remains the innocent exercise of the freedom of speech.

Once all of the above is clear, we can now demonstrate that Islām, the Prophet Muḥammad (صَلَّى ٱللَّهُ عَلَيْهِ وَسَلَّمَ) and the Muslims at large are free and innocent of the terrorists, their evil ideology and their evil actions.

---

[81] Aḥmad in *al-Musnad* (no. 8729).

[82] As has preceded, Muslims are prohibited from abusing and mocking the deities of others, even though have the right to do so upon the alleged absolute principle of the freedom of speech. But the Qur'ān has prohibited Muslims from engaging in such practices in order to prevent escalation and violation of sanctities.

Muḥammad (صَلَّىٰ ٱللَّهُ عَلَيْهِ وَسَلَّمَ) Against The Terrorists

Allāh (عَزَّوَجَلَّ) stated in what He revealed to Muḥammad (صَلَّىٰ ٱللَّهُ عَلَيْهِ وَسَلَّمَ) - and this verse was interpreted by the Prophet's Companions to be in reference to **the Khārijite terrorists** when they appeared and killed the best of the Muslims:[83]

قُلْ هَلْ نُنَبِّئُكُم بِٱلْأَخْسَرِينَ أَعْمَٰلًا ﴿١٠٣﴾ ٱلَّذِينَ ضَلَّ سَعْيُهُمْ فِى ٱلْحَيَوٰةِ ٱلدُّنْيَا وَهُمْ يَحْسَبُونَ أَنَّهُمْ يُحْسِنُونَ صُنْعًا

> **Say: Shall we inform you of the greatest losers as to [their] deeds? Those whose efforts have been wasted in this life while they thought that they were acquiring good by their deeds!** (18:103-104).

It is common knowledge to most Muslims of the world today, their scholars, students and even lay people that **ISIS, Boko Ḥarām and al-Qāʿidah** are from the group that was explicitly mentioned by the Prophet of Islām. They are known as **the Khārijites (extremist renegades).** They have killed exponentially more Muslims in the past 1400 years than they have killed non-Muslims in the past 20 years. In fact, if we were to say this the other way around, that they have killed more Muslims in the past 20 years than they have killed non-Muslims in the past 1400 years it would not be an exaggeration at all.[84] Their appearance was prophesized by the Prophet (صَلَّىٰ ٱللَّهُ عَلَيْهِ وَسَلَّمَ) in a large number of traditions and they indeed appeared less than 30 years after him in 36-37H, around the year 657CE. Because this faction was intended as a trial and tribulation for Muslims in various times and ages, the Prophet (صَلَّىٰ ٱللَّهُ عَلَيْهِ وَسَلَّمَ) spoke extensively about them, their traits,

[83] Refer to the opening section of Imām al-Shāṭibī's excellent work, *al-Iʿtiṣām*.

[84] This is because the Khārijites revolt against Muslim authorities and their subjects. Their activities are primarily directed towards them and not non-Muslims. Refer to the articles from Der Spiegel and the Washington Times later in this book which review statistical research on this subject.

activities and their great danger upon Islām and the Muslims. The traditions in this regard are well-known and famous.

MATTERS OF WEALTH ARE THEIR PRIMARY MOTIVATION

The primary motivation driving Khārijite extremists returns back to matters of wealth and how Muslim rulers dispose of it. The ideological grandfather of all Khārijite renegade movements in Islāmic history is a man known as **Dhul-Khuwaiṣarah al-Tamīmī**. This man challenged the integrity of the Prophet (صَلَّى ٱللَّٰهُ عَلَيْهِ وَسَلَّمَ) as famously documented in numerous Prophetic traditions.[85] As the Prophet (صَلَّى ٱللَّٰهُ عَلَيْهِ وَسَلَّمَ) was distributing wealth to a number of tribes for certain benefits he had in mind for them, this man appeared and said, "Be just O Muḥammad" and "We are more worthy of this than them" and also, "This is a division by which the pleasure of Allāh is not sought."[86] The Prophet (صَلَّى ٱللَّٰهُ عَلَيْهِ وَسَلَّمَ) had to prevent his Companions from striking this audacious man and as the man walked away, the Prophet (صَلَّى ٱللَّٰهُ عَلَيْهِ وَسَلَّمَ) said, "*From this man's offspring will appear a people who recite the Qur'an but it will not go beyond their throats.*"

[85] The Qur'ān judged this individual to be from the disbelieving hypocrites, "**Amongst them (the Hypocrites) is one who criticizes you concerning the [distribution of] charities. If they are given from them, they approve but if they are not given from them, at once they become angry**." (9:58). During the incident in question, ʿUmar (رَضِيَ ٱللَّٰهُ عَنْهُ) was present and referred to the man as a hypocrite.

[86] Refer to al-Bukhārī (nos. 3610 and 4351). This is proof that the entire issue with the Khāriijte terrorists is a worldly one and relates to wealth. They are discontent with how the rulers acquire and dispose of wealth. Using the religion as a vehicle, they seek to acquire power themselves to control both land and wealth and through this evil methodology, they bring destruction and chaos. One can see here the parallels between the ideology of the Khārijites and the Marxist, Communist movements. Once this similarity is identified no shock and surprise will remain when one discovers that all 20th century takfīrī, jihādī, revolutionary movements have their basis in the ideas and writings of men who were engrossed in European materalist philosophies at some stage in their lives - from them Sayyid Quṭb and Taqī al-Dīn al-Nabahānī, the founder of Ḥizb al-Tahrīr.

THE PROPHET'S CHARACTERIZATION OF THE KHĀRIJITE TERRORISTS

From the well-known, authentically related statements of the Prophet (صَلَّى ٱللَّٰهُ عَلَيْهِ وَسَلَّمَ) about this group[87] include his saying, "*They depart from the religion (Islām) like an arrow passes through its game*" and "*Their faith does not pass beyond their throats*" and "*They recite the Qur'ān but it does not go beyond their collar-bones,*" indicating ignorance and false scholarship. He (صَلَّى ٱللَّٰهُ عَلَيْهِ وَسَلَّمَ) also said, "*They speak with the best speech of the creation,*" meaning, beautified, alluring speech, and "*(They are) young of age, foolish of mind*" and "*Their speech is beautiful, alluring yet their actions are evil*" and "*They are the most evil of the creation*" and "*They call to the Book of Allāh, yet they have nothing to do with it.*" The Prophet (صَلَّى ٱللَّٰهُ عَلَيْهِ وَسَلَّمَ) went further and also said "*They are the most evil of those killed beneath the canopy of the sky*" and "*They are the Dogs of Hellfire.*"

THEIR CONTINUED APPEARANCE THROUGHOUT TIME

The Prophet (صَلَّى ٱللَّٰهُ عَلَيْهِ وَسَلَّمَ) indicated that they will not cease to appear in every age and era by saying, "*There will emerge a people from my nation from the East who recite the Qur'ān but it does not go beyond their throats. Every time a faction amongst them emerges it will be cut off. Every time a faction amongst them emerges it will be cut off,*" until he said this ten times, (and then he said) "*Every time a faction amongst them emerges it will be cut off, until the Dajjāl (Anti-Christ) appears amongst their (later) remnants.*"[88] The Salafī scholar, Shaykh ʿAbd al-Muḥṣīn al-ʿAbbād commented on this tradition by saying, "He (Dajjāl) will be with them and they will be with him."[89] An indication that the Khārijites, from their beginning to their end, are at war with the people of Islām.

---

[87] These reports can be found in the ḥadīth collections of al-Bukhārī, Muslim, Abū Dāwūd, Ibn Mājah and others and are well known and famous to the Scholars of the Muslims, the students of knowledge and many of the common folk. It is great oppression therefore, that the actions of these terrorists are ascribed to Islām and its noble Prophet (صَلَّى ٱللَّٰهُ عَلَيْهِ وَسَلَّمَ).

[88] Related by Ibn Mājah.

[89] In his recorded lessons of commentary upon *Sunan Ibn Mājah.*

THE COMMAND TO FIGHT AND KILL THEM

The Prophet (صَلَّىٱللَّهُعَلَيْهِوَسَلَّمَ) encouraged the Muslim rulers to fight them whenever they appear with their turmoil and bloodshed. He said, "*Wherever you meet them, kill them, for there is a reward on the Day of Judgement for whoever kills them.*" And he also said, "*If I was to reach them, I would slaughter them, like the slaughtering of ʿĀd (a destroyed nation of the past),*" meaning, every last one of them until not one of them remains as explained by the classical Scholar, Ibn Ḥajar al-ʿAsqalānī in his commentary on this tradition.[90] For this reason, the Muslim rulers from the time of the fourth righteous Caliph **ʿAlī bin Abī Ṭālib** (رَضِيَٱللَّهُعَنْهُ) have never ceased to fight against them. When they appeared, the Companions of the Prophet (صَلَّىٱللَّهُعَلَيْهِوَسَلَّمَ) applied the aforementioned Qurʾānic verse upon them: Misguided in this life and losers in the next because their deeds were vain whilst they deceived themselves into thinking they were doing good.

TERRORISM AGAINST THE PROPHET'S COMPANIONS

Their first act of terrorism was against the Companion of the Prophet called **ʿAbdullāh bin Khabbāb** (رَضِيَٱللَّهُعَنْهُ) near Baṣrah in Irāq in the year 37H. Despite giving him assurance of safety at the first encounter, they acted treacherously towards him when they excommunicated him because he did not agree with their position that ʿAlī, the fourth caliph and cousin of the Prophet, was an apostate. Thereafter, they laid him on the ground and slaughtered him whilst his blood flowed into the nearby water stream. Then they murdered his woman who was at the peak of pregnancy. She pleaded for her life and that of her unborn child, but they sliced her open and spared not even her child. Then they killed numerous others who were present in his caravan.[91] It was here that the cousin and son-in-law of the Prophet, **ʿAlī bin Abī Ṭālib** (رَضِيَٱللَّهُعَنْهُ) followed the Prophetic traditions ordering this group to

[90] Refer to *Fatḥ al-Bārī* (6/435).

[91] This incident is related by numerous historians such as al-Ṭabarī and Ibn al-Athīr and others.

be fought and killed. It should be noted that groups such as **ISIS, Boko Ḥarām and al-Qaidah** are the ideological descendants of those very first Khārijite terrorist renegades and had the noble, esteemed, lofty, honourable, merciful Prophet of Islām (ﷺ) been alive to reach them and their likes, he would have slaughtered them until not a single one of the savages remained. The Khārijite terrorists are a trial for the Muslims before they are a trial for anyone else. This has been transmitted century after century in the written works of the Muslim scholars. It is common knowledge amongst the students and many of the common-folk and none but the Khārijite savages resent the conveyance of these traditions which convict them and their evil.

THEY MURDERED THE PROPHET'S COUSIN AND SON-IN-LAW

The Khārijites appeared as a distinct faction when they broke off from the army of **ʿAlī bin Abī Ṭālib** (رَضِيَ اللَّهُ عَنْهُ), the Prophet's cousin and son-in-law. They accused him of becoming an apostate because he authorized an arbitration by which reconciliation was intended between himself and another party led by the famous companion known as Muʿāwiyah (رَضِيَ اللَّهُ عَنْهُ). Due to their severe ignorance and the absence of a single scholar amongst them, the Khārijites held this arbitration to be an act of disbelief because in their misguided view it entailed judging by other than Allāh's law. Hence, they excommunicated the Companions and split away from the main body of Muslims. It was only after their murder of ʿAbdullāh bin Khabbāb that ʿAlī bin Abī Ṭālib (رَضِيَ اللَّهُ عَنْهُ) recognized these were the very people spoken of by the Prophet (ﷺ) decades earlier and mobilized himself to fight them.[92] A number of years after battling them, one of the extremist Khārijites called ʿAbd al-Raḥmān bin Muljam plotted to assassinate ʿAlī (رَضِيَ اللَّهُ عَنْهُ) and attained his evil objective in the year 40H (661CE). This is the way of these people throughout the ages until this day of ours: To pursue

---

[92] Shaykh Muḥammad bin ʿAbd al-Wahhāb (d. 1206H, 18th century CE) said, "When ʿAlī (رَضِيَ اللَّهُ عَنْهُ) reached Kūfah, the Khārijites revolted against him and declared him a disbeliever for being satisfied with the arbitration." *Mukhtaṣar Ṣīrah al-Rasūl* in *Majmūʿ Muʾallafāt al-Shaykh* (1/222).

wealth and power by undermining the Islāmic authorities and bringing chaos, destruction and bloodshed through murder, assassination, terror and chaos. In the Prophetic traditions, the Muslim rulers are commanded to fight these Khārijites whenever they appear because their evil ideology and terrorist mindset is the first of enemies to the religion of Islām and runs contrary to it from every angle. The Mufti of Saudi Arabia, Shaykh ʿAbd al-ʿAzīz Āl al-Shaykh remarked, "The terrorism of ISIS is the very first enemy of Islām."[93] The leaders amongst them are motivated by wealth, land, power and politics and simply use Islām as a hijacked vehicle or a donned, beautified garment through which they pursue worldly interests. They recruit the young, ignorant and foolish. Whilst the noble, just, Prophet of Islām, Muḥammad (ﷺ) commanded that these evil and most harmful of people to Islām and its adherents be fought, killed and cut off we see on the other hand that they and their activities are most beneficial in serving the agendas of those who oppressively ascribe their activities to the Prophet of Islām (ﷺ). This is despite the historical record showing that the Prophet of Islām (ﷺ) was challenged by their ideological grandfather, Dhul Khuwayṣarah, that his Companions were slaughtered and murdered by them and that the Islāmic tradition throughout history is squarely against them.

THE SECT OF THE AZĀRIQAH: FORERUNNERS OF ISIS

Many early Islāmic scholars from the 3rd, 4th and 5th centuries of Islām who specialized in the study of deviant sects (heresiography) documented the beliefs and actions of one of the most extreme sects of the Khārijite terrorists known as **the Azāriqah**. ISIS are reminiscent of this group.[94] Their founder was Abū Rāshid Nāfiʿ bin Azraq (d. 65H around 685CE). The Azāriqah split off from the Khārijites and made their way to Baṣrah, taking control over it and other areas in Persia.

[93] This was covered in many leading Arabic newspapers in August 2014. Refer to http://arabic.cnn.com/middleeast/2014/08/19/saudi-mufti-isis.

[94] Refer to *al-Milal wal-Niḥal* of al-Shahrastānī (1/112).

Their evil doctrines included the belief that the excommunication of ʿAlī (رَضِيَ اللَّهُ عَنْهُ) was valid and correct and that Ibn Muljam, the assassin, was praiseworthy. In their view, all sinful Muslims are apostates who will reside in Hellfire for eternity should they die without having repented from their sins.[95] Whoever opposed their opinion was considered a polytheist and they threw the children of such people alongside them - all of them were considered disbelievers whom it was permissible to fight and kill. The land inhabited by those outside their group was considered to be land of war (*dār al-ḥarb*) and whatever was permitted with respect to a land of war was permitted to them against the Muslims inhabiting such a land. Anyone who did not join them by emigrating to them *even if he held their view* was considered a polytheist. They also held the necessity of eliminating every "disbeliever" from the Earth, and by "disbeliever" they mean every Muslim who does not agree with them. They would interrogate Muslims on their views towards the rulers.[96] They would lay in wait for Muslims, slaughter them and also slaughter their children mercilessly, on the flimsiest of grounds until they instilled terror in the hearts of civilians.

Many of the ideas of this extreme sect can be found today amongst the Khārijite terrorists of ISIS in the land of Shām (Syria) and Irāq - **the very place** from which the Prophet of Islām indicated, over 1400 years ago, that these people would first emerge after his death and continue to emerge through the ages.[97] In the tradition related by Abū

[95] This clashes with the belief of orthodox Muslims who hold that the sinful amongst the Muslims who die without repentance will be eventually delivered due to their pure monotheism.

[96] Whoever did not agree with their excommunication of the Muslim rulers of the time would be killed.

[97] Many Islāmic scholars and students of knowledge have spoken or authored in order to establish the similarity between the doctrines of ISIS and those of the Khārijites of old. When the statements of the leaders and spokesmen of ISIS and videos of activities of their members which are publicly available are compared with those of the very first Khārijites, no other conclusion can be made except that they are the very *Khārijite Dogs of Hellfire* mentioned and

Sa'īd al-Khudrī, the Prophet (صَلَّى ٱللَّٰهُ عَلَيْهِ وَسَلَّمَ) said, "*There will appear a people from the East, they will recite the Qur'ān and it will not pass beyond their throats...*"[98] and in the tradition related by Yasīr bin 'Āmr who said that he asked Sahl bin Ḥunayf, "Did you hear the Prophet (صَلَّى ٱللَّٰهُ عَلَيْهِ وَسَلَّمَ) say anything about the Khārijites?" Sahl said that he heard the Prophet saying - and Sahl pointing his hand towards Irāq - "*There will appear from there a people who recite the Qur'ānn, it will not pass beyond their throats, and they will depart from Islām like the arrow passes through the game.*"[99]

ISLĀMIC SCHOLARS ON THE KHĀRIJITES THROUGHOUT THE AGES

In another tradition, the **Prophet Muḥammad** (صَلَّى ٱللَّٰهُ عَلَيْهِ وَسَلَّمَ) said, "*There will appear at the end of time*[100] *a people who are young of age, foolish-minded. They will speak with the best (and most-alluring) of speech (that is spoken) by people and will recite the Qur'ān but it will not go beyond their throats. They will pass out of Islām as the arrow passes through its game. Whoever meets them, let him kill them, for there is a reward for whoever kills them.*"[101] The Prophet's Companion, **Abū Umāmah al-Bāhilī** (رَضِيَ ٱللَّٰهُ عَنْهُ) said of the Khārijites, "The Dogs of the people of Hellfire, they used to be Muslims but turned disbelievers." When Abū Umāmah was asked whether this was his own speech or something he heard from the Prophet, he said, "Rather, I heard it from the Prophet (صَلَّى ٱللَّٰهُ عَلَيْهِ وَسَلَّمَ)."[102] **Qatādah** (d. 118H, 8th century CE), the famous Qur'anic commentator, said about them as cited by Imām al-Ṭabarī, "The Khārijites emerged whilst the Companions of Allāh's Messenger (صَلَّى ٱللَّٰهُ عَلَيْهِ وَسَلَّمَ) were plentiful in al-Madīnah, Shām and 'Irāq, and his wives were still alive. By Allāh,

---

intended by the Prophetic traditions. This prophecy about the Khārijites is one of many serving as proof for the truthfulness of the Prophet (صَلَّى ٱللَّٰهُ عَلَيْهِ وَسَلَّمَ).

98 Related by al-Bukhārī (no. 7652).

99 Related by al-Bukhārī (no. 6934).

100 The various Prophetic traditions about them indicate that they were to appear shortly after the death of the Prophet (صَلَّى ٱللَّٰهُ عَلَيْهِ وَسَلَّمَ) and would continue to appear through the passing of time, putting the Muslims to trial.

101 Reported by Ibn Mājah (no. 167).

102 Reported by Ibn Mājah (no. 175).

none of them (the Companions), male or female, came out as a Ḥarūrī (Khārijite) ever, and they were not pleased with what they (the Kharijites) were upon, nor did they support them in that. Rather, they used to convey the criticism by Allāh's Messenger (ﷺ) of them and the descriptions with which he described them. They used to hate them with their hearts and would show enmity towards them with their tongues. By Allāh, their hands would be severe against them whenever they came across them."[103] This proves that Islām has always been in one direction and the Khārijite terrorists have been in an altogether different direction. There was not a single companion of the Prophet with them, showing that they departed completely from the main body of Islām.

Imām al-Ṭabarī (d. 310H, 10th century CE) said, "The Khārijites would meet each other and remember the location (of battle) of their brothers [of old] at al-Nahrawān. They held that remaining stationary amounted to cheating and weakness and that in [the activity of] making jihād against the Muslims (*ahl al-qiblah*) lay excellence and reward."[104] **Imām al-Ājurrī** (d. 360H, 10th century CE) said in his book entitled *The Sharīʿah*, "It is not permissible for the one who sees the uprising of a Khārijite who has revolted against the leader, whether [the leader] is just or oppressive - so this person has revolted and gathered a group behind him, has pulled out his sword and has made lawful the killing of Muslims - it is not fitting for the one who sees this, that he becomes deceived by this person's recitation of the Qurʾān, the length of his standing in prayer, nor his constant fasting, nor his good and excellent words in knowledge when it is clear to him that this person's way and methodology is that of the Khārijites."[105] We see that this speech of this insightful scholar is not heeded today by the ignorant and youthful who are deceived by the apparent display of what is really fake piety by the Khārijites of ISIS and rush to join them in their evil. **Ibn Ḥazm al-Andalūsī** (d. 456H, 11th century

[103] *Tafsīr al-Ṭabarī*, Dar Iḥyā al-Turāth al-ʿArabī, 1421H, 3/209

[104] *Tārikh al-Ṭabarī* (5/174).

[105] *Al-Sharīʿah* (p. 28).

CE) said, "And they do not cease to strive in overturning the orderly affairs of the Muslims (to chaos) and splitting the word of the believers. They draw the sword against the people of religion and strive upon the Earth as corrupters. As for the Khārijites and Shīʿah, their affair in this regard is more famous than that one should be burdened in mentioning."[106] **Ibn Taymiyyah** (d. 728H, 14th century CE) said, "For they [the Khārijites] strived to kill every Muslim who did not agree with their view, declaring the blood of the Muslims, their wealth, and the slaying of their children to be lawful, while excommunicating them. And they considered this to be worship, due to their ignorance and their innovation that caused [them] to stray."[107] **Ibn Kathīr**, the famous Qurʾān commentator, (d.774H, 14th century CE) said, "If these [Khārijites] were to acquire strength, they would corrupt the entire earth in Irāq and Shām (Syria) and they would not leave a male or female child nor a man or woman (alive). This is because in their view the people (Muslims) have become corrupt in a way that nothing will rectify their (situation) except mass murder."[108] **Shaykh ʿAbd al-ʿAzīz bin Bāz** (d. 1419H, 20th century CE) the former muftī of Saudi Arabia stated, "That which is apparent from the Prophetic traditions is that they are disbelievers." He also said, after mentioning the view of the scholars who consider the Khārijites to be sinful, astray Muslims, "That which is correct is that they are disbelievers," citing as evidence the statement of the Prophet, "*If I was to reach them, I would slaughter them like the slaughtering of ʿĀd.*" The people of ʿĀd were nation of the past who belied their Prophet and were destroyed by a screaming, violent wind without a single survivor. Shaykh Ibn Bāz then said, "The correct and apparent view from the textual evidences is that on account of their extremism, their expulsion of Muslims (from the fold of Islām) and declaring them to be eternal inhabitants of Hellfire, they are disbelievers."[109]

---

106 *Al-Faṣl Fil-Milal al-Ahwāʾ wal-Niḥal* (5/98).
107 *Minhāj us-Sunnah* (5/248).
108 *Al-Bidāyah wal-Nihāyah* (10/585).
109 http://www.binbaz.org.sa/mat/20688.

THE MUSLIMS DO NOT BENEFIT FROM TERRORISM AT ALL

Today, ISIS and al-Qaidah, their ideology and their activities are as alien to Islām and its people as were their predecessors, the Khārijite renegade extremists who embarked upon murdering the Prophet's Companions. Terrorists such as Usāmah bin Lādin, al-Qā'idah and ISIS do not serve the interests of Muslims, their governments, nations or lands. Thus, the maligning of Islām and its Prophet by the lying, fraudulent, oppressive pencil of the cartoonist raises questions about who truly benefits from the existence and activities of these terrorists. In reality, when we get through the fog and the mist, the activities of the cartoonist and the terrorist proceed in parallel to facilitate the heaping of lies upon Islām, it's Prophet and the Muslims in general. This raises the question as to whose interests are being served by the activities of the Khārijites. The Muftī of Saudī Arabia, Shaykh ʿAbd al-ʿAzīz Āl al-Shaykh recently said, "I doubt they are Muslims (in truth)... they are under dubious banners (of leadership) in which there is no goodness." and "The terrorism of ISIS is the very first enemy of Islām."[110] And he also said, "These factions (of Khārijites) are nurtured under (the pens) of global intelligence agencies."[111] It should now be clear that actions of terrorism, destruction and chaos founded upon a twisted, evil ideology is the very first enemy to Islām and its people and is most detrimental to them in more than one way. Thus, scapegoating all Muslims for this evil is gross injustice. In light of this, we are now in a position to demonstrate that Prophet Muḥammad (صَلَّىٰللَّهُعَلَيۡهِوَسَلَّمَ) is exonerated from the false accusations of the liars, the evil insinuations of the mockers, and that their mockery falls back upon themselves in reality, "**And already were Messengers ridiculed before you, but those who mocked them were enveloped by what they used to ridicule.**" (21:41).

---

[110] This was covered in many leading Arabic newspapers in August 2014. Refer to http://arabic.cnn.com/middleeast/2014/08/19/saudi-mufti-isis.

[111] Refer to http://www.youtube.com/watch?v=TmuNHYRQkCQ. More than one notable scholar from Ahl al-Sunnah has expressed this view.

The Prophet and His Followers Have Been Sufficed Against the Mockers

Allāh (عَزَّوَجَلَّ) stated in what He revealed to Muḥammad (صَلَّىٰللَّهُعَلَيْهِوَسَلَّمَ):

إِنَّا كَفَيْنَٰكَ ٱلْمُسْتَهْزِءِينَ

Indeed, We are sufficient for you against the mockers. (68:4)

When the Prophet of Islām, Muḥammad (صَلَّىٰللَّهُعَلَيْهِوَسَلَّمَ), peacefully invited to the same message of all of the Prophets of the Children of Isra'īl (Jacob) before him -[to abandon the worship of stones, trees, the elements, the forces, causes and effects, animals, prophets or the righteous or any created entities and to reserve it only for the creator of all entities, beings forces, causes and effects] - those who felt threatened by this simple message consisting of no more than *a few words*[112] embarked upon a sustained campaign of hindrance, abuse, mockery, physical harm, repeated assassination attempts and declarations of war to hinder him from speaking.

This took place over a period of 23 years. The story is a long one but Islamophobes driven by irrational hate omit a large portion of the story so as to give the impression that Muḥammad (صَلَّىٰللَّهُعَلَيْهِوَسَلَّمَ) was a murderous maniac. Orientalist scholars such as Bernard Lewis dispelled the myth that Islām was spread by the sword (see his book *The Jews of Islām*) as did many other writers throughout the 19th and 20th centuries such as Thomas Carlyle,[113] Lawrence Browne,[114] James Michener,[115] De Lacy O'Leary[116] and others.[117]

---

112 *Lā ilāha illallāh*, the statement professed by all the Prophets of God.

113 "Our current hypothesis about Mahomet, that he was a scheming Impostor, a Falsehood incarnate, that his religion is a mere mass of quackery and fatuity, begins really to be now untenable to any one. The lies, which well-meaning zeal has heaped round this man, are disgraceful to ourselves only." In *On Heroes, Hero-worship and the Heroic in History*.

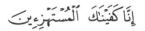

Today, we live in the world of the tube, social media and cartoons. One can falsify and distort established history in an instance through the use of satire and mockery which is founded upon lies not facts. Most people do not have the motivation or the means to ascertain the claims and simply enjoy the cheap satirical humour. Only the most-blatant of liars and hatemongers get caught out and justifiably ridiculed. How fine an example there is in Mr. Steven Emerson[118] and his Fox News host Jeanine Pirro[119] in this regard.

---

[114] "Incidentally these well-established facts dispose of the idea so widely fostered in Christian writings that the Muslims, wherever they went, forced people to accept Islam at the point of the sword." *The Prospects of Islām* (1944).

[115] "No other religion in history spread so rapidly as Islam. The West has widely believed that this surge of religion was made possible by the sword. But no modern scholar accepts this idea." *Reader's Digest*, May 1955, pp. 68-70.

[116] "History makes it clear, however, that the legend of fanatical Muslims sweeping through the world and forcing Islam at the point of sword upon conquered races is one of the most fantastically absurd myths that historians have ever repeated." In *Islam at the Crossroads*, London, (1923).

[117] Whilst most of them rose above medieval prejudices they did not entirely escape from bias and contradictions in their accounts. Nevertheless, they tried to be as objective as possible and that's a far throw from the Islamophobes of today.

[118] This "terrorism" expert is one of many who spread hatred against Islām and the Muslims with evil propaganda. Mr Emerson displayed sub-zoology intelligence when in the wake of the Paris attack he said that Birmingham city (in the UK) is entirely Muslim and is a no go area for non-Muslims. He was ripped and torn to pieces via Twitter, mercilessly, by both non-Muslims and Muslims alike until he was forced to make an uncompromising apology. You can analogize with Mr. Emerson for other "terrorism" experts who are either paid shills for spewing propaganda, grossly ignorant or malicious haters. Refer to the excellent piece of research, "**Fear Inc. the Roots of the Islamophobia Network in America**" which exposes the well-orchestrated, well-funded network of hate that is used to shape public opinion against Muslims in the US. Another report, "**The Cold War on British Muslims**" highlights the existence of a similar network in the UK. Both can be found via online search and details are at the end of this book.

[119] Jeanine Pirro led Mr. Emerson in the interview through directed questions and made certain remarks indicating her role as hatemongress during the interview, "You know what it sounds like Steve, it sounds like a caliphate

Most mass-media outlets (print or digital) are *privately owned*. There is no obligation upon their owners to tell the truth to anyone. Politically motivated opinions are broadcast and presented in such a way that the audience is left to assume they are facts. This allows the views and opinions of the audience to be shaped and manipulated. In turn the beneficial interests of the private owners of that mass media or whoever they serve can be realized more easily. Mocking the Prophet (صَلَّى ٱللَّٰهُ عَلَيْهِ وَسَلَّمَ) and ridiculing Islām is part of that agenda whereby Muslims are deliberately provoked and agitated. The terrorist, as misguided and evil his action already is, plays into the hands of such a hostile media which is operated to fulfil agendas and thus becomes a servant to its cause. The cartoonist and the terrorist aid each other in working against Islām and its people and they both serve the same master.

So let us go back to the **bomb in the turban myth** and concisely deal with it. The polytheists of Quraysh - when their idol-worship and monopoly over society was threatened by a simple statement[120] - began to ridicule Muḥammad (صَلَّى ٱللَّٰهُ عَلَيْهِ وَسَلَّمَ) by accusing him of being a poet, a soothsayer, a magician, a madman and one to whom stories are dictated. When this failed to hinder people from Islām, they began persecuting and torturing his followers over a period of many years. The first martyr was a woman, Sumayyah (رَضِيَ ٱللَّٰهُ عَنْهَا), an elderly, barren woman who was killed by Abū Jahl with a spear. Muslims were forced on a number of occasions to emigrate to Abysinnia to flee from persecution.[121] When the approach of torture and murder towards the

---

within a particular country" and "Steve is there any way to get these no zones back. In other words does France want them back, does Belgium want them back, does Germany want these zones back, because what's happening is this is metastasizing into a simple takeover." Pirro issued an apology days later, not for the hatemongering she clearly participated in but for the "serious factual error" her guest made regarding Birmingham city as a no go zone for non-Muslims.

[120] *Lā ilāh illallāh* (There is none worthy of worship in truth but Allāh alone).

[121] **Muslim Emigrations to Negus the Christian King.** After the second wave of emigration, the pagans of Quraysh sent two delegates to King Negus of Abyssinia to convince him to return the Muslims upon the argument that

they were not upon the religion of the Quraysh and nor upon the religion of Negus (Christianity) but had innovated a new religion and were nothing but fools. Al-Najāshī was a cautious and just man, so he decided to hear the view of the Muslims. He summoned them and asked about this religion which they were practising. Jaʿfar bin Abī Ṭālib, the cousin of the Prophet Muḥammad, representing the Muslims, said, "O King, we were a people of ignorance. We used to worship idols, eat (the meat of the) dead animal, we would perform shameless deeds, cut off the ties of kinship, ill-treat the neighbour and the strong amongst us would devour the weak. This is what we used to be upon until Allāh sent us a messenger from amongst ourselves. We know his lineage, his truthfulness, his trustworthiness and his chastity. He called us to single out Allāh [in His lordship] and to worship Him alone. That we abandon what we and our forefathers used to worship besides Him of stones and idols. He ordered us to be truthful in speech, to fulfil our trusts, to join the ties of kinship, to be good to the neighbour, to withhold from the prohibited sanctities and shedding of blood. He forbade us from shameless deeds, giving false witness, consuming the wealth of the orphan, falsely accusing chaste women (of indecency) and ordered us to worship Allāh alone and not associate any partners with Him. He ordered us with prayer, obligatory charity and fasting - and other affairs of Islām. So we attested to his truthfulness, believed in him, followed that which he came with, worshipped Allāh alone and did not associate any partners with Him. We treated as unlawful what Allāh made unlawful and we treated as lawful what Allāh made lawful. So then our people transgressed against us, they punished us and put us to trial with respect to our religion in order to make us revert to the worship of idols, away from the worship of Allāh, and so that we declare lawful what we used to previously consider lawful of vile things. When they subdued us, oppressed us, made life difficult for us and came in between us and our religion, we left our land and chose you over others. We desired your proximity and hoped that we would not be oppressed in your presence, O King." When Negus heard this, he requested Jaʿfar to recite something from the Qur'ān and Jaʿfar read the opening verses of the nineteenth chapter, called "Maryam" which recounts the story of Zakariyā, John, Mary and Jesus (عَلَيْهِمُالسَّلَامُ). Upon hearing the Qur'ān being recited, Negus cried profusely until his beard became wet with tears and those around him also cried. Then Negus said, "Indeed this and what Jesus came with has emanated from the same lamp." Then Negus addressed the two delegates of the pagans of Quraysh and said to them, "Be off! For by Allāh, we shall not deliver (these Muslims) to you." Refer to *Rawḍat al-Anwār Fī Sīrah al-Nabī al-Mukhtār* of al-Mubārakfūrī (pp. 48-49). There are many benefits and lessons in this incident for Muslims who live in the non-Muslim lands such as the UK, US, Europe,

Prophet's followers failed they began to physically harm the Prophet himself, something they avoided previously because of his nobility in lineage and standing in society. When this approach failed they resorted to assassination attempts. During all this time the Prophet (ﷺ) was ordered to continue preaching peacefully and to endure their harm, without any retaliation. When the assassination attempts increased, he was forced to migrate to what became the city of al-Madīnah. Tensions grew as the Muslim convert numbers increased and emigrations to al-Madīnah took place in stealth. The polytheists entered into alliances with each other in order to murder the Prophet (ﷺ) and wipe out the small fledgling Muslim community. Throughout this period, Muḥammad (ﷺ) was ordered to incline towards peace, avoid war at every possibility and exhaust the avenues of conciliation, restraint, truces and treaties. Failing all of this, permission was given to the Muslims to defend themselves. In these battles they fought face to face with a type of fighting in which the full meaning of **bravery, courage and valour** were retained unlike the cowardice of modern warfare in which bombs are dropped from the sky killing very large numbers instantly. This honourable fighting was enjoined to help remove obstacles so that people could hear the message peacefully, without hindrance.[122] An accurate correlation between the verses pertaining to jihād and the facts of history in the Prophetic biography will inform the truth-seeking reader of these

---

Canada and Australia where they live in relative security and are free to practice Islām. It is from the greatest treachery that covenants and contracts of peace and security are broken through acts of aggression and terrorism in these lands. These acts are in complete opposition to the spirit of Islām in which the fulfilment of contracts and covenants is the greatest of obligations. Violating them is from the most special signs of hypocrisy (*nifāq*) and indicative of the lack of genuine faith.

[122] Forced conversions are prohibited in Islām and as the scholar, Ibn al-Qayyim mentioned, the Prophet Muḥammad (ﷺ) never forced a single person to convert to Islām. He fought those who waged war against him and hindered him from peacefully preaching his message. As for the claim of a universal, indefinite jihād against every non-Muslim and the claim that peaceful preaching has been abrogated, this is erroneous as pointed out by Ibn Taymiyyah and others. See later in the book.

realities and will inform the reader that the Prophet's mission was to educate and guide and not to murder and kill.[123] The leaders of the Western nations in particular know that it was not the actions of the Prophet of Islām or any Muslim government that led to the death of 17 million people in the First World War or over 60 million in the Second World War with airplanes, guided missiles, tanks, machine guns and horrendous chemical warfare using poison gas. Muslims did not develop and drop the A-bomb on Hiroshima and Nagasaki, killing 200,000 men, women and children through incineration and its after effects. Nor was it Muslims who killed 2 million Vietnamese with bombs and napalm over a period of ten years.[124]

The first picture shows one of many mass graves that were continuously being discovered in Japan decades after the A-bomb was dropped. The second picture is a scene from the aftermath of the Hiroshima bombing showing thousands of dead littered on the streets. We have given only a few examples, the list could go on and on. The intelligent person understands the point straight away and will be thinking of many other instances in which souls were carpet-bombed, mustard-gassed, napalmed or white-phosphorused into

[123] The relevant texts pertaining to jihād are often distorted and mentioned out of context by Islam haters. Refer to the section on Jihād in this book.

[124] It can be argued through atheistic existentialist philosophies that there is nothing morally wrong in these actions because ultimately, life is **inherently meaningless, insignificant and purposeless** and **no sound basis** exists to assert absolute moral values. Hence, these actions cannot be judged immoral and wrong in the overall scheme of things in such a world view.

liberation, but not by Muslims. **There was and is no bomb in the turban.** That's pure cartoon fiction for sub-zoology minds. Many Orientalists of the 19th and 20th centuries only barely managed to throw off the shackles of medieval prejudice and started writing a bit more objectively about Islām and its noble Prophet (صَلَّى ٱللَّٰهُ عَلَيْهِ وَسَلَّمَ). Then came American Fox News, Pope Joseph Ratzinger, Danish cartoons and French substandard, cheap satire magazines only to return back to the medieval ages of superstitious fabrications. What a great and profound statement of fact it is that, "Muḥammad (صَلَّى ٱللَّٰهُ عَلَيْهِ وَسَلَّمَ) and his rightly-guided Caliphs and his noble Companions did not erect factories for the manufacture of elementary weapons such as swords and spears, let alone atomic bombs and missiles and other such wholly destructive weapons. Muḥammad (صَلَّى ٱللَّٰهُ عَلَيْهِ وَسَلَّمَ) did not erect a single factory because he was sent as a mercy to the worlds, to guide all of mankind to that which brings them happiness in the world and afterlife."[125]

Let's leave the last word for Jewish secular atheist, Uri Avnery who wrote:[126] "In his lecture at a German university, the 265th Pope described what he sees as a huge difference between Christianity and Islam: while Christianity is based on reason, Islam denies it. While Christians see the logic of God's actions, Muslims deny that there is any such logic in the actions of Allah. As a Jewish atheist, I do not intend to enter the fray of this debate. It is much beyond my humble abilities to understand the logic of the Pope. But I cannot overlook

125 Islāmic scholar, Shaykh Rabīʿ bin Hādī in *al-Intiṣār lil-Rasūl al-Mukhtār* (2006) being a response to Pope Ratzinger's slander against the Prophet (صَلَّى ٱللَّٰهُ عَلَيْهِ وَسَلَّمَ). Weapons industries are not the specialization of Muslims. All the innovative and technological ways to kill hundreds, thousands or hundreds of thousands with advanced weapons in an instant, the industries built around this business model, the associated factories and ancillary businesses are not owned by Muslims. Islām does not enjoin upon its followers to turn war and the death of millions into a profitable business model. That's the way of the nihilists, warmongers and nation-destroyers to whom human life holds little value.

126 In an article titled *Muḥammad's Sword*, 26th September 2006.

one passage, which concerns me too, as an Israeli living near the fault-line of this 'war of civilizations.' In order to prove the lack of reason in Islam, the Pope asserts that the Prophet Muhammad ordered his followers to spread their religion by the sword." After speaking about Muslim Spain, Avnery then writes, "Every honest Jew who knows the history of his people cannot but feel a deep sense of gratitude to Islam, which has protected the Jews for fifty generations, while the Christian world persecuted the Jews and tried many times 'by the sword' to get them to abandon their faith. The story about 'spreading the faith by the sword' is an evil legend, one of the myths that grew up in Europe during the great wars against the Muslims - the reconquista of Spain by the Christians, the Crusades and the repulsion of the Turks, who almost conquered Vienna. I suspect that the German Pope, too, honestly believes in these fables. That means that the leader of the Catholic world, who is a Christian theologian in his own right, did not make the effort to study the history of other religions."[127] End of quote. In short, the lofty, honourable, noble Prophet of Islām (صَلَّى ٱللَّٰهُ عَلَيْهِ وَسَلَّمَ) is sufficed from mockery, not by terrorism, treachery and violation of contracts, which is unlawful in the Islāmic legislation, but by the brute force of cold hard facts and dignified patience and forbearance in the face of mockery and abuse founded upon nothing but vicious lies.

---

[127] The view of Avnery is echoed by many just and honest religious figures amongst the Jews, from their learned Rabbis, and the citations in this regard are numerous and plentiful. For a glimpse at how Jews fared under Muslim rule one can refer to *A History of the Jewish People* edited by Haim Hillel Ben-Sasson, Harvard University Press (1985). It is a comprehensive book written by six Jewish scholars from Hebrew University in Jerusalem for Jewish readers and spans 5000 years of history. A consistent pattern emerges from the book that throughout Islāmic history Jews have fared well and lived in comfortable conditions. A sample quote from the book, "The height of magnificence and luxury was reached by the wealthy Jews in the lands of Islam, particularly in Moslem Spain. We know that the court bankers of Baghdad in the tenth century kept open house for numerous guests and for the poor. Similarly, the ceremonies of the Jewish leaders in Babylonia and the patronage of the leading Jews in Moslem Spain, indicate conditions of ease and plenty." (p.401)

Prophet Jesus (عَلَيْهِ السَّلَام), the Klu Klux Klan and Rupert Murdoch

The heads of Western states, politicians, officials, diplomats and influential people in all areas of life (including Rupert Murdoch)[128] are asked to ponder over the following and to perform a little thought experiment. If a satirical magazine such as Charlie Hebdo was to publish a cartoon mocking the Prophet Jesus (عَلَيْهِ السَّلَام) by attributing the crimes and racism of the **Klu Klux Klan** to him or the massacre of children by the Norwegian Christian **Anders Brevik**[129] or the terrorism of the **Catholic IRA**, a large portion of the world (at the head of them would be Muslims),[130] numerous heads of state and religious figures would have risen in uproar and the wicked, malicious intent of the perpetrators of this humongous lie would have felt the fiery brunt of their anger and indignation.

This is because all people of learning would know this to be a lie, a fabrication, motivated by malicious intent and not the principle of the *freedom of speech*. With that said, the noble, honourable, revered Prophet of Islām, Muḥammad (ﷺ) has been sufficed against lies

---

[128] In a tweet dated 9th January 2015, following the Paris attacks, Rupert Murdoch stated that all Muslims should be held responsible for the attacks. He backtracked days later when he was mocked and humiliated from many different directions.

[129] Anders Brevik, who revealed himself in his writings as an extremist right-wing Christian Zionist, massacred around 80 or so youth members of a pro-Palestinian Labour Youth Party Group whilst they were on an island retreat in Norway in July 2011. Breivik cited US-based anti-Muslim extremists dozens of times in his manifesto, including Pamela Geller and Robert Spencer, two hate-filled loons and co-founders of *Stop Islamization of America.*

[130] This is because the Prophet Jesus (عَلَيْهِ السَّلَام) holds the loftiest of positions in the heart of every Muslim and because Muslims have a greater right to Jesus than those who oppose the message of Islām he came with, deified him and worshipped him and his mother as gods besides Allāh (عَزَّوَجَلَّ) - something he never called to and which clashes with the fundamental message he came with, that none has the right to be worshipped but God alone.

and mockery and his elevated mention will not be lowered, neither by the pencil of the cartoonist nor the evil distortion of the terrorist, for the Prophet of Islām is free and innocent of the claims of both groups. His message is alien to the ideology and activity of the Khārijites just as his message is innocent of the lies and insinuations of the spiteful nihilists.

Whoever ascribed the actions of the ISIS, Boko Ḥarām or al-Qā'idah terrorist to Muḥammad (صَلَّى ٱللَّهُ عَلَيْهِ وَسَلَّمَ) is the same as the one who ascribes the racism and "negro"-lynching of the Klu Klux Klan, the terrorism of the IRA and the massacre of 80 or so youth by Anders Brevik to Jesus (عَلَيْهِ ٱلسَّلَامُ). Both are wicked liars in the judgement of all people of sound mind, integrity and justice.

The intent here is to illustrate that Jesus (صَلَّى ٱللَّهُ عَلَيْهِ وَسَلَّمَ) is free and innocent of the crimes which are done by those who acribe to him or which are done in his name.[131] Further, that to mock and revile Muḥammad (صَلَّى ٱللَّهُ عَلَيْهِ وَسَلَّمَ) because of the actions of the Khārijite terrorists whom he himself expelled from Islām[132] *and* declared his intent to slaughter them should he have reached them is no different to making mockery and revilement of Jesus (عَلَيْهِ ٱلسَّلَامُ) and attributing to him the murder of hundreds of millions of native American Indians, Africans, Australians and Asians and others in genocides committed by Christian European nations and their leaders over the past few hundred years.

---

[131] Worthy of note is the fact that IRA terrorism was never labelled as "Catholic Terrorism" and the massacre by Anders Brevik, a Christian white Norwegian who murdered 80 or so youth members of the Labour Youth Party Movement at an island gathering in Norway has never been identified as a "Christian Terrorist" in digital mass-media or print press. Rupert Murdoch's newspapers however, were quick to label the Brevik incident as an "Al-Qaeda Massacre" in big bold red letters on the front page in the immediate aftermath of the event before the truth about the massacre began to emerge with the passing of hours.

[132] As is the view of many credible Islāmic scholars, past and present.

Europe, Genocidal Holocausts and the Pope

For a period of five centuries from 1492[133] right into the mid-20th century, European nations such as Portugal, Spain, France, Britain, Holland, Belgium, Germany and Italy employed colonization, terrorism, brutal violence, evangelization and implementation of economic and trade policies, often within the context of environmental disasters (such as famines), with a view to hastening the demise of the indigenous populations in the colonized lands and enriching their own empires. These activities were justified on grounds of racial superiority, the "glory of Christ" and a God-given right to rule over inferior races. The large gap in technology and industry between European countries and the natives of America, Africa, Asia and Australia often afforded Europeans the great advantage of possessing advanced weapons. Such weapons proved effective in "pacification" of natives and wiping out indigenous populations. Today, when the cartoonist in Europe draws a satirical caricature of the Prophet Muḥammad (صَلَّى ٱللَّٰهُ عَلَيْهِ وَسَلَّمَ) by which offense and deliberate provocation is intended or when Pope Ratzinger claims that Prophet Muḥammad (صَلَّى ٱللَّٰهُ عَلَيْهِ وَسَلَّمَ) spread Islām by the sword, it has to involve an active deed of forgetting Europe's history of mass murder, terrorism and genocide across four continents of the world. Likewise, when many of the leaders of the world behave as if the right to slander and revile the Prophet Muḥammad (صَلَّى ٱللَّٰهُ عَلَيْهِ وَسَلَّمَ) by attributing the crimes of Khārijite terrorists to him is the *ultimate test* of the principle of the freedom of speech, it has to involve a conscious and active deed of forgetting the mass murder, terrorism and genocide justified by either white Christian supremacism or 19th and 20th century European secular, materialist pseudoscience.

---

[133] Christopher Columbus did not *discover* America, it was already inhabited by people for thousands of years. Colonial history was of course written by the colonialists and most people have a romantic picture of benevolent Europeans setting out to civilize people. The reality is far from it and can be glimpsed through many academic publications in this regard which reveal that self-enrichment and empire-expansion was the primary objective.

A large number of books and academic research papers are available regarding these affairs of history.[134] In what follows, we will take a look at perhaps the largest, sustained, long-term genocide in history and the nature of its relevance to our discussion.

THE AMERICAN HOLOCAUST BY DAVID STANNARD

American Holocaust: Columbus and the Conquest of the New World was published in 1992 by Oxford University Press.[135] Just as it is ludicrous to assert that Hitler did not engage in eugenics and racially motivated genocidal practices against minorities, it is also ludicrous to assert

[134] One can refer to *King Leopold's Ghosts* by Adam Hochschild who discusses this Belgian king's genocide of 10 million Congolese over a 23 year period at the end of the 19th century. There is also a documentary with the same name as the book. Another documentary titled *White King, Red Rubber, Black Death* by Peter Bates can also be viewed online. The book by Mike Dave, *Late Victorian Holocausts* is a study of imperialism in the 19th century and its policy of maximizing revenue at the expense of tens of millions of lives. *Churchill's Secret War* is another eye-opening book by Madhusree Mukerjee which reveals the deliberate genocide of four million Bengal Indians during 1939 to 1944. Carol Elkin's *Britain's Gulag*, David Anderson's *Histories of the Hanged* and Mark Curtis' *Web of Deceit* are all good reads on the subject of the use of terror and mass murder in dispossessing people of their lands. For a concise review of the well-researched literature on European colonial terrorism and premeditated genocide in American, African and Australian continents refer to the numerous papers written by Asafa Jalata, Professor of Sociology at the University of Tennessee, Knoxville.

[135] Vanderbilt University published a lecture by the author on Youtube under the title "*American Holocaust: The Destruction of America's Native Peoples*." The description of the video contains the following information, "American Holocaust: The Destruction of America's Native Peoples, a lecture by David Stannard, professor and chair of the American Studies Department at the University of Hawaii. Stannard, author of American Holocaust, asserts that the European and white American destruction of the native peoples of the Americas was the most substantial act of genocide in world history. A combination of atrocities and imported plagues resulted in the death of roughly 95 percent of the native population in the Americas. Stannard argues that the perpetrators of the American Holocaust operated from the same ideological source as the architects of the Nazi Holocaust."

that what happened in the Americas at the hands of Christopher Columbus and others after him was not genocide. David Stannard explores the main cultural and religious traditions that paved the way for mass murder on huge scales in the Americas.

EXCERPTS FROM THE AMERICAN HOLOCAUST

The following are a number of passage from the chapter on *Pestilence and Genocide* in Stannard's book:

"Following Columbus, each time the Spanish encountered a native individual or group in the course of their travels they were ordered to read to the Indians a statement informing them of the truth of Christianity and the necessity to swear immediate allegiance to the Pope and the Spanish crown. After this, if the Indians refused or even delayed in their acceptance or more likely, their understanding of the Requerimiento, the statement continued: 'I certify to you that, with the help of God, we shall powerfully enter into your country and shall make war against you in all ways and manners that we can, and shall subject you to the yoke and obedience of the Church and of Their Highnesses. We shall take you and your wives and your children, and shall make slaves of them, and as such shall sell and dispose of them as Their Highnesses may command. And we shall take your goods, and shall do you all the mischief and damage that we can, as to vassals who do not obey and refuse to receive their lord and resist and contradict him.' In practice, the Spanish usually did not wait for the Indians to reply to their demands. First the Indians were manacled; then, as it were, they were read their rights. As one Spanish conquistador and historian described the routine: 'After they had been put in chains, someone read the

Requerimiento without knowing their language and without any interpreters, and without either the reader or the Indians understanding the language they had no opportunity to reply, being immediately carried away prisoners, the Spanish not failing to use the stick on those who did not go fast enough.' In this perverse way, the invasion and destruction of what many, including Columbus, had thought was a heaven on earth began. Not that a reading of the Requerimiento was necessary to the inhuman violence the Spanish were to perpetrate against the native peoples they confronted. Rather, the proclamation was merely a legalistic rationale for a fanatically religious and fanatically juridical and fanatically brutal people to justify a holocaust. After all, Columbus had seized and kidnapped Indian men, women, and children throughout his first voyage, long before the Requerimiento was in use, five at one stop, six at another, more at others, filling his ships with varied samples of Indians to display like exotic beasts in Seville and Barcelona upon his return."[136]

A little later, Stannard writes: "Spanish reports of their own murderous sadism during this time are legion. For a lark they 'tore babes from their mother's breast by their feet, and dashed their heads against the rocks.' The bodies of other infants 'they spitted... together with their mothers and all who were before them, on their swords.' On one famous occasion in Cuba a troop of a hundred or more Spaniards stopped by the banks of a dry river and sharpened their swords on the whetstones in its bed. Eager to compare the sharpness of their blades, reported an eyewitness to the events, they drew their weapons and '...began to rip open the bellies, to cut and kill those lambs - men, women, children, and old folk, all of whom were seated, off guard and frightened, watching the mares and the Spaniards. And within two credos, not a man of all of them there remains alive. The Spaniards enter the large house nearby, for this was happening at its door, and in the same way, with cuts and stabs, begin to kill as many

[136] Refer to *American Holocaust*, (pp. 65-67).

as they found there, so that a stream of blood was running, as if a great number of cows had perished... To see the wounds which covered the bodies of the dead and dying was a spectacle of horror and dread.' This particular slaughter began at the village of Zucayo, where the townsfolk earlier had provided for the conquistadors a feast of cassava, fruit, and fish. From there it spread. No one knows just how many Indians the Spanish killed in this sadistic spree, but Las Casas put the number at well over 20,000 before the soldiers' thirst for horror had been slaked. Another report, this one by a group of concerned Dominican friars, concentrated on the way the Spanish soldiers treated native infants: 'Some Christians encounter an Indian woman, who was carrying in her arms a child at suck; and since the dog they had with them was hungry, they tore the child from the mother's arms and flung it still living to the dog, who proceeded to devour it before the mother's eyes.... When there were among the prisoners some women who had recently given birth, if the new-born babes happened to cry, they seized them by the legs and hurled them against the rocks, or flung them into the jungle so that they would be certain to die there.' Or, Las Casas again, in another incident he witnessed: 'The Spaniards found pleasure in inventing all kinds of odd cruelties, the more cruel the better, with which to spill human blood. They built a long gibbet, low enough for the toes to touch the ground and prevent strangling, and hanged thirteen [natives] at a time in honor of Christ Our Saviour and the twelve Apostles. When the Indians were thus still alive and hanging, the Spaniards tested their strength and their blades against them, ripping chests open with one blow and exposing entrails, and there were those who did worse. Then, straw was wrapped around their torn bodies and they were burned alive. One man caught two children about two years old, pierced their throats with a dagger, then hurled them down a precipice.' If some of this has a sickeningly familiar ring to readers who recall the massacres at My Lai and Song My and other Vietnamese villages in the not too distant past, the familiarity is reinforced by the term the Spanish used to describe their campaign of terror: 'Pacification.' But as horrific as those bloodbaths were in

Vietnam, in sheer magnitude they were as nothing compared with what happened on the single island of Hispaniola five hundred years ago: The island's population of about eight million people at the time of Columbus's arrival in 1492 already had declined by a third to a half before the year 1496 was out. And after 1496 the death rate, if anything, accelerated."[137]

Stannard writes a few pages later: "The gratuitous killing and outright sadism that the Spanish soldiers had carried out on Hispaniola and in Central Mexico was repeated in the long march to the south. Numerous reports, from numerous reporters, tell of Indians being led to the mines in columns, chained together at the neck, and decapitated if they faltered. Of children trapped and burned alive in their houses, or stabbed to death because they walked too slowly. Of the routine cutting off of women's breasts and the tying of heavy gourds to their feet before tossing them to drown in lakes and lagoons. Of babies taken from their mothers' breasts, killed, and left as roadside markers. Of 'stray' Indians dismembered and sent back to their villages with their chopped-off hands and noses strung around their necks. Of 'pregnant and confined women, children, old men, as many as they could capture,' thrown into pits in which stakes had been imbedded and 'left stuck on the stakes, until the pits were filled.' And much, much more. One favorite sport of the conquistadors was 'dogging.' Traveling as they did with packs of armored wolfhounds and mastiffs that were raised on a diet of human flesh and were trained to disembowel Indians, the Spanish used the dogs to terrorize slaves and to entertain the troops. An entire book, *Dogs of the Conquest*, has been published recently, detailing the exploits of these animals as they accompanied their masters throughout the course of the Spanish depredations. 'A properly fleshed dog,' these authors say, 'could pursue a 'savage' as zealously and effectively as a deer or a boar.... To many of the conquerors, the Indian was merely another savage animal, and the dogs were trained to pursue and rip apart their

[137] Refer to *American Holocaust*, (pp.70-75).

human quarry with the same zest as they felt when hunting wild beasts.' Vasco Nunez de Balboa was famous for such exploits and, like others, he had his own favorite dog - Leoncico, or 'little lion,' a reddish-colored cross between a greyhound and a mastiff-that was rewarded at the end of a campaign for the amount of killing it had done. On one much celebrated occasion, Leoncico tore the head off an Indian leader in Panama while Balboa, his men, and other dogs completed the slaughter of everyone in a village that had the ill fortune to lie in their journey's path. Heads of human adults do not come off easily, so the authors of *Dogs of the Conquest* seem correct in calling this a 'remarkable feat,' although Balboa's men usually were able to do quite well by themselves. As one contemporary description of this same massacre notes: 'The Spaniards cut off the arm of one, the leg or hip of another, and from some their heads at one stroke, like butchers cutting up beef and mutton for market. Six hundred, including the cacique, were thus slain like brute beasts. ...Vasco ordered forty of them to be torn to pieces by dogs.' Just as the Spanish soldiers seem to have particularly enjoyed testing the sharpness of their yard-long rapier blades on the bodies of Indian children, so their dogs seemed to find the soft bodies of infants especially tasty, and thus the accounts of the invading conquistadors and the padres who traveled with them are filled with detailed descriptions of young Indian children routinely taken from their parents and fed to the hungry animals. Men who could take pleasure in this sort of thing had little trouble with less sensitive matters, such as sacking and burning of entire cities and towns, and the destruction of books and tablets containing millennia of accumulated knowledge, wisdom and religious belief."[138] End quote.

Pope Joseph Aloisius Ratzinger who accused the Prophet Muḥammad (صَلَّىٱللَّهُعَلَيْهِوَسَلَّمَ) of spreading Islām by the sword does not do history for obvious reasons, or perhaps he pretends not to do history for sinister reasons.

---

138 Refer to *American Holocaust*, (pp.80-84).

IN ISLĀM NO BEARER OF BURDENS BEARS THE BURDEN OF ANOTHER

Alongside the point just made, it is equally important to clarify that no Muslim who is upon the correct orthodox interpretation of Islām will judge the rulers or individual subjects of European nations with the atrocities committed by those who passed before them. Certainly that is not the point and nor the objective behind recounting the details which have preceded. Muslims have been ordered with justice and not to speak except the truth. Allāh (عَزَّوَجَلَّ) states in His Book, **"That is a nation which has passed on. It will have [the consequence of] what it earned, and you will have what you have earned. And you will not be asked about what they used to do."** (2:134).[139] And He also said, **"And no bearer of burdens will bear the burden of another."** (53:38). Indeed, there are many large-scale atrocities that have taken place in the history of the world besides those perpetrated by European nations, and the child or descendant of no criminal is to be held accountable for the criminal actions of his father or forefathers - this is a fundamental, solid Islāmic precept. Within this principle is a refutation of those who harbour enmity and hatred towards non-Muslim societies *because* of the deeds of their ancestors. Instead of inviting such societies to the beauty of Islām through knowledge, exemplary conduct, benevolence and wisdom, they are motivated by historical grudges based on matters of land, wealth or nationalistic fervor - in stark opposition to the way of the Prophet (صَلَّىٰللَّهُعَلَيْهِوَسَلَّمَ). One can refer to the incident of Ṭā'if whose mention has preceded wherein the Prophet (صَلَّىٰللَّهُعَلَيْهِوَسَلَّمَ) was cast out of the city and stoned by children at the behest of its leaders. Despite that, he never took revenge or wished for their destruction. Leaving them alone, he hoped that their offspring in future generations might turn out better than them.

---

[139] Shaykh ʿAbd al-Raḥmān bin Nāsir al-Saʿdī, a 20th century Salafī scholar, commented upon this Qurʾānic verse by saying, "Each person has their own action and each person will be recompensed with what he did. No one will be held accountable for the crime of anyone else..." Refer to his commentary in *Taysīr al-Karīm al-Raḥmān*. In Islām, one cannot hold grudges against a son for the crime of his father, let alone the crimes of his bygone ancestors.

This shows that Islām came with guidance for mankind and not their destruction. Intelligent thinking people appreciate these truths and see both fallacy and hypocrisy in the Danish cartoons which depict Prophet Muḥammad (ﷺ) with a bomb in his turban and in the rantings of Pope Ratzinger who claimed Islām was spread by the sword.[140] Thus, the Prophet (ﷺ) is sufficed against these baseless lies and such lies only encompass those who spread them.

---

[140] Whilst it is certainly true that Islam being spread by forced conversion with the sword is a myth and that whole nations accepted Islām without a single Arab soldier setting foot in their lands such as Indonesia and most of Malaysia, it is also true that Muslims did conquer lands through military means. However, their armies were relatively small in size making forced conversions of entire nations impossible. Dr. Paul Kennedy, British historian at Yale University, writes in his paper, "*Was Islam Spread by the Sword?*" that much of the conquest was through treaty. Further, people in the conquered lands had a whole host of reasons to convert besides "*fear of the Moozlems.*" In many nations the common people were weak, exploited and oppressed and they anticipated better treatment from Muslims whose honesty, integrity, justice and good character they had heard of. Millions converted just through interactions with Muslims alone, after observing their utmost honesty in trade and their noble, impeccable manners. Wherever Muslims went, the indigenous populations remained the overwhelming majority. Christian and Jewish communities were littered all across the Muslim lands. Had there been forced conversions, these communities would have been non-existent. In many cases, communities fled Christian rule in order to live under a more just Muslim rule due to their certainty that they would receive better treatment. In a Los Angeles Times article, William Montalbano writes, "The Jews of Istanbul, who have lived for centuries along the shores of the Golden Horn, never tire of one particular sea story: In 1492, Christopher Columbus set sail from the tiny port of Palos... because the harbors at Cadiz and Seville were jammed with boatloads of Sephardic Jews expelled from Spain by his royal sponsors. Columbus went west to uncertainty. Around 60,000 Jews exiled that year by Ferdinand and Isabella came east to official welcome in lands of the Ottoman Empire. Thousands more joined them after an interim stop in Portugal. Now, their Turkish descendants are preparing a year-long celebration of a Jewish tradition that since the 15th Century has flourished in an Islamic universe... 'We want to send the world a message that we have been living here peacefully for centuries while other Jewish communities have suffered in many lands of Europe,' said Sami Kohen..." *For Jews, a 500-Year Turkish Haven*, Los Angeles Times, 2nd November 1991.

Muḥammad (صَلَّى ٱللَّهُ عَلَيْهِ وَسَلَّمَ): Most Influential Figure in History

Of all figures in history whose mockery could have been chosen as *the ultimate test* for *freedom of expression,* Muḥammad (صَلَّى ٱللَّهُ عَلَيْهِ وَسَلَّمَ) is perhaps singled out for a reason: He is the exemplary model for well over a billion Muslims who may be perceived, *in at least some xenophobic and Islamophobic quarters*, in the same way as those native American Indians were perceived and portrayed by the European perpetrators of genocidal holocausts in bygone centuries or as the Congolese were viewed by King Leopold II[141] or as Churchill viewed the Indians, red or brown. The Prophet (صَلَّى ٱللَّهُ عَلَيْهِ وَسَلَّمَ) is sufficed against such mockery and the nobility and truth of his message stands on its own right and is not affected by such cheap attempts at denigration and ridicule. Allāh (عَزَّ وَجَلَّ) ordered His Prophet to pronounce the essence of his call, that which led him to be the greatest and most influential man on Earth:

قُلْ إِنَّمَآ أَنَا۠ بَشَرٌ مِّثْلُكُمْ يُوحَىٰٓ إِلَىَّ أَنَّمَآ إِلَٰهُكُمْ إِلَٰهٌ وَٰحِدٌ ۖ فَمَن كَانَ يَرْجُوا۟
لِقَآءَ رَبِّهِۦ فَلْيَعْمَلْ عَمَلًا صَٰلِحًا وَلَا يُشْرِكْ بِعِبَادَةِ رَبِّهِۦٓ أَحَدًۢا ﴿١١٠﴾

> **Say (O Muḥammad to mankind): "I am only a man like you. It has been inspired to me that your deity is but one deity alone (who is worthy of worship). So whoever hopes for the meeting with his Lord, let him work righteousness and associate none as a partner in the worship of his Lord."** (18:110).

No amount of **materialist** or **existentialist** brainwashing can remove the innate, pre-programmed intuitive belief that the universe and its order, regularity and design indicate an existence beyond it. Sound reason corroborates this. Amazement at the universe and its workings

141 The Belgian King who was responsible for the death of at least 10 million Congolese between 1885 and 1908. Mark Twain satirized him in "*King Leopold's Soliloquy: A Defence of His Congo Rule*" - a work that is not public knowledge and nor readily publicized unlike *Huckleberry Finn* and *Tom Sawyer*.

compel honest souls to the belief that there is a will beyond it and that it is not all in vain, without purpose. By appeal to this intuition, along with reason and revelation, the Messenger Muḥammad (صَلَّى ٱللَّٰهُ عَلَيْهِ وَسَلَّمَ) - as did all of the Messengers before him such as Abraham, Moses and Jesus (عَلَيْهِمُ ٱلسَّلَامُ) - demonstrated that the worship of stones, trees, the elements, the forces, the planets, stars, the sun, the moon, causes and their effects, animals, prophets or the righteous or any created entities is futile in intuition, common sense, sensory perception, reason and revelation. On that basis they invited mankind to show exclusive devotion and gratitude only to the Creator of the elements, entities, forces and intertwined systems of cause and effect that the universe is comprised of and through which innumerable benefits are brought to every living creature. The entire universe appears designed to facilitate life and indicates a purpose and meaning (to life) leading to a foundation for moral codes. Each soul has been inspired with a conscience and an inherent, basic sense of morality to make it inclined towards wholesome, beneficial conduct. Upon this scheme of things, the Prophets, themselves upright and moral,[142] called to a perfection of morals and manners centered around this underlying foundation of Tawḥīd (pure monotheism). Through the morality they enjoined - which allows for attainment of pleasure through sex between males and females within marriage[143] - the institution of marriage and the family became the fabric of society through which stable, mentally sound, morally upright, disciplined and mindful individuals are produced. The legislation of Islām which

---

[142] All of the Prophets and Messengers were upright and lead moral lives. As for what is claimed against some of the Prophets of God, then it is either a lie in its foundation or a distortion of the scripture. Muslims do not affirm the veracity of the claims in distorted scripture against the Prophets of the Children of Isrāʿīl. The Qurʾān exonerates the Prophets from the fabrications made against them and considers all of them to be upright.

[143] Had there been anything morally objectionable in the conduct of Prophet Muḥammad (صَلَّى ٱللَّٰهُ عَلَيْهِ وَسَلَّمَ) his enemies would have used these matters to discredit him and expose him before anything else. However, his greatest enemies, many of whom tried to kill him for at least a decade could not find an iota against his morals and manners, because there was nothing culturally, morally or religiously objectionable in his conduct at all.

the Prophet conveyed, is aimed at protecting certain necessities which include the preservation of life, lineage, honour and wealth. Thus, usury is strictly forbidden and is considered a war against God before it is considered a war against society. Marriage is the context within which sexual relations take place and the attainment of such pleasures are tied to responsibility. The law of retribution is aimed at protection of life. All intoxicants are prohibited. The legislation of Islām brought **perfection of balance** between **the rights of the individual** and **the rights of society** and **protection of all beneficial interests**. It enjoined or commended everything whose benefit to society as a whole overwhelmed its harm and outlawed everything whose harm to society as a whole overwhelmed its benefit. In what he called to and established, Muḥammad (صَلَّى ٱللَّٰهُ عَلَيْهِ وَسَلَّمَ) is the leader of the Muslims and also the leader of mankind in his influence, piety, humility, uprightness, morals and manners. This is testified to by numerous non-Muslim scholars and academics.[144]

John William Draper, (d. 1882), American scientist, philosopher, and historian, wrote, "Four years after the death of Justinian, A.D. 569, was born at Mecca, in Arabia the man who, of all men, exercised the greatest influence upon the human race... Mohammed."[145] **William Montgomery Watt** (d. 2006), Professor (Emeritus) of Arabic and Islamic Studies at the University of Edinburgh, wrote, "His readiness to undergo persecutions for his beliefs, the high moral character of the men who believed in him and looked up to him as leader, and the greatness of his ultimate achievement - all argue his fundamental

---

[144] One should note that most non-Muslim writers tend to evaluate the life of Muḥammad (صَلَّى ٱللَّٰهُ عَلَيْهِ وَسَلَّمَ) on the basis of worldly standards and achievements without considering him to be a genuine Prophet of God. While this is a clear testimony to the loftiness of the person of Muḥammad (صَلَّى ٱللَّٰهُ عَلَيْهِ وَسَلَّمَ) even by their standards, some specific writers did not refrain from conveying misconceptions, inaccuracies or even lies about the Prophet (صَلَّى ٱللَّٰهُ عَلَيْهِ وَسَلَّمَ).

[145] *A History of the Intellectual Development of Europe*, 1875, vol.1, pp. 329-330. Draper's view is also expressed by others who list Muḥammad (صَلَّى ٱللَّٰهُ عَلَيْهِ وَسَلَّمَ) as the most influential man in history, above all other famous people, be they kings, philosophers, leaders, reformists, scientists or religious figures.

integrity. To suppose Muhammad an impostor[146] raises more problems than it solves. Moreover, none of the great figures of history is so poorly appreciated in the West as Muhammad."[147] **Washington Irving** (1783-1859), American author and diplomat, wrote, "He was sober and abstemious in his diet, and a rigorous observer of fasts. He indulged in no magnificence of apparel, the ostentation of a petty mind; neither was his simplicity in dress affected, but the result of a real disregard to distinction from so trivial a source... In his private dealings he was just. He treated friends and strangers, the rich and poor, the powerful and the weak, with equity, and was beloved by the common people for the affability with which he received them, and listened to their complaints... His military triumphs awakened no pride nor vain glory, as they would have done had they been effected for selfish purposes. In the time of his greatest power he maintained the same simplicity of manners and appearance as in the days of his adversity. So far from affecting regal state, he was displeased if, on entering a room, any unusual testimonial of respect were shown to him."[148] **Ramakrishna Rao**, Hindu professor of Philosophy writes, "The personality of Muhammad, it is most difficult to get into the whole truth of it. Only a glimpse of it I can catch. What a dramatic succession of picturesque scenes. There is Muhammad the Prophet. There is Muhammad the Warrior; Muhammad the Businessman; Muhammad the Statesman; Muhammad the Orator; Muhammad the Reformer; Muhammad the Refuge of Orphans; Muhammad the Protector of Slaves; Muhammad the Emancipator of Women; Muhammad the Judge; Muhammad the Saint.[149] All in all these magnificent roles, in all these departments of human activities, he is like a hero."[150] **Alphonse de Lamartine** (d. 1869), French poet and statesman, wrote,

---

[146] Mongomery Watt has indicated here the problem that many Orientalists and academics who wrote about Muḥammad (ﷺ) encounter when they question the integrity of the Prophet.

[147] *Mohammad At Mecca*, Oxford, 1953, p. 52.

[148] *Life of Mahomet*, London, (1889), pp. 192-3, 199.

[149] In Islām the concepts of "sainthood" or "holiness" do not exist. These are Christian concepts comprising exaggeration which lead to worship of men.

[150] In his work, *Muḥammad the Prophet of Islām*,

"Philosopher,[151] orator, apostle, legislator, warrior, conqueror of ideas, restorer of rational dogmas, of a cult without images; the founder of twenty terrestrial empires and of one spiritual empire, that is Muhammad. As regards all standards by which human greatness may be measured, we may well ask, is there any man greater than he?"[152] **Edward Gibbon** (d. 1794), the famous British historian, wrote, "The greatest success of Mohammad's life was effected by sheer moral force without the stroke of a sword."[153] **Annie Besant** (d. 1933), British socialist, wrote "It is impossible for anyone who studies the life and character of the great Prophet of Arabia, who knows how he taught and how he lived, to feel anything but reverence for that mighty Prophet, one of the great messengers of the Supreme. And although in what I put to you I shall say many things which may be familiar to many, yet I myself feel whenever I re-read them, a new way of admiration, a new sense of reverence for that mighty Arabian teacher."[154] **David George Hogarth** (d. 1927), English archaeologist author and keeper of the Ashmolean Museum, Oxford, wrote, "Serious or trivial, his daily behaviour has instituted a canon which millions observe this day with conscious mimicry. No one regarded by any section of the human race as Perfect Man has been imitated so minutely. The conduct of the Founder of Christianity has not so governed the ordinary life of His followers. Moreover, no Founder of a religion has been left on so solitary an eminence as the Muslim Apostle."[155] Muḥammad (صَلَّى ٱللَّهُ عَلَيْهِ وَسَلَّمَ), the Prophet of Islām has been praised by these writers for his outstanding, virtuous qualities and his achievements. These writers are certainly not in the same league as the immoral cartoonists of today. This now leads us to the French prophet of Existentialism, a philosophy which underpins the outlook in many aspects of Western culture and secular, liberal societies.

---

[151] Muḥammad (صَلَّى ٱللَّهُ عَلَيْهِ وَسَلَّمَ) was not a philosopher. His teachings were not from his own thought, opinion and reason. Rather, his speech was revelation inspired by God and even the pagan Arabs were unable to deny this.

[152] A translated excerpt from *Histoire De La Turquie*, Paris, 1854.

[153] *History Of The Saracen Empire*, London, 1870.

[154] *The Life And Teachings Of Muhammad*, Madras, 1932, p. 4.

[155] In his book, *Arabia*, Oxford, 1922, p. 52

Jean-Paul Sartre, Prophet of Existentialism

A faction similar to the modern Existentialist nihilists are mentioned in the Qurʾān. There used to be amongst the polytheist Arabs those who denied resurrection and accountability after death. Allāh (عَزَّوَجَلَّ) cites their statement in the Qurʾān: **And they say: "There is nothing but our life of this world, we die and we live and nothing destroys us except the passing of time." And they have no knowledge of it, they only conjecture.** (45:24). In opposition to the Prophets and Messengers who receive revelation for the rectification of societies and establishment of **objective moral standards**, the philosophies of most philosophers are simply rational justifications for living the life they have decided is most beneficial or pleasurable to them in light of the subjective experiences they have encountered in their personal lives. One such outlook (religion) is Existentialism, its 20th century prophet was the French philosopher, **Jean-Paul Sartre**. He died in 1980 and 50,000 people turned up on the streets of Paris. We have seen the Prophet Muḥammad (صَلَّىٱللَّهُعَلَيْهِوَسَلَّمَ) characterized in the words of intelligent, honest academics, famous historians and other than them. Their words are in stark contrast to what is found in the cartoons of those motivated by hate before they are motivated by the alleged principle of *freedom of speech*. But it is interesting to see for what ideas people like Sartre are celebrated and how they lived their personal lives. Jean-Paul Sartre was **a serial seducer**. His philosophy paved the way for others to live private lives of **utter depravity**.[156] Sartre's ideas were explored in his novels and philosophical works for which he was given the Nobel Prize. He had an open relationship with **Simone de Beauviour** who was fired from her teaching job in 1943 for seducing her female students. Her and Sartre had an agreement that they would remain committed to each other in a kind of "union" whilst allowing **unlimited sexual relationships** with others outside of their "union." They were both serial seducers who used their philosophy for gratification and exploitation of children, many of whom were psychologically harmed by the disturbing experiences they were put

[156] Refer to *A Dangerous Liaison: Simone de Beauvoir and Jean-Paul Sartre*, Carole Seymour-Jones (2008).

through. Jealousies would make them retaliate against each other. Simone would sleep with men and Sartre would retaliate by sleeping with girls and their sisters. Both would then recount to each other the sordid details of their escapades. Simone de Beauvoir, who was a feminist, hated marriage and family. She would recruit her pupils, exploit and abuse them and then pass them on to Sartre for joint pleasure. Girls were groomed by Beauvoir so Sartre could take their virginity and Sartre's rationale was that these girls would be "empowered" by the experience. The reader should note that these permissive philosophies (whose propounders and practitioners such as Sartre utilized to justify private lives of depravity outside the tradition of marriage) played a role in helping to shape the negative perception towards what had been a normal and standard practice in many cultures and civilizations for thousands of years: Marriage between adults of any age (where the attainment of adulthood was marked by puberty)[157] with the full involvement of the parental or legal guardians of the bride. When the practitioners of this philosophy engaged in actions of exploitation and fornication - at a time when

[157] In the 19th century, the usual age of consent in the US was ten years and in the state of Delaware until the mid 1960s it was seven years. Prior to the 20th century children were mentally mature at a much younger age and the onset of puberty was seen as a direct graduation into adulthood. The notion of *adolescense* is a new one and appeared in the early 20th century. Biological adulthood is not the same as *legal* adulthood. Sinikka Elliot writes, "As the United States grew increasingly urbanized in the late 1800s, young people were gradually removed from their role in the labour force and were conceptualized as innocent and vulnerable. The statutes governing the minimum age under which sex cannot be legally consensual, and laws concerning marriage and workers' rights, were modified to reflect these changing discourses around childhood. Age of sexual consent, for example rose from 7 during colonial times to 10, 12, and even as high as 14 during the eighteenth and nineteenth centuries." *Not My Kid* (2012) pp. 14-15. Professor of History, Margaret Wade Labarge writes, "It must be remembered that many medieval widows were not old. Important heiresses were often married between the ages of 5 and 10 and might find themselves widowed while still in their teens." A Medieval Miscellany (1997), p.52. Due to changes in the social and economic milieu, today's children remain children for much longer and do not attain maturity until a much later age thereby wedging a large gap between the age of puberty and the age of mental maturity.

children had long been removed from those roles which traditionally made them reach mental maturity and adulthood much earlier in life - other intellectuals defended these actions under the banner of *sexual liberation.*[158] Thus one should note the difference between the standard practice of marriage between adults of any age in cultures and civilizations for thousands of years and the depravity justified through existentialist, nihilist philosophies and *sexual liberation movements.* In short, materialism and existentialism comprise **a religion** with its own prophets, dogmas and **subjective morality**. Atheists resent the Prophets of God and under the slogan of "*freedom of speech*" denigrate them, their teachings and moral codes whilst defending and glorifying their own morally bankrupt prophets of nihilism. Whilst the **terrorist**, operating upon a twisted, corrupt and evil ideology, destroys society in a particular way using twisted logic, evil rhetoric, weapons and bombs. The **extreme liberal and permissive existentialist nihilist** destroys society in another way. The terrorist attempts to throw upon the Prophet (ﷺ) what justifies his own evil. The existentialist nihilist tries to makes his own path look liberating and illuminating. The Prophets of God are innocent of them both for the Prophets are rectifiers, not destroyers.

---

[158] As an illustration, in 1977, around seventy French intellectuals and politicians signed a petition seeking to abolish all age of consent laws (for sex). Michel Foucault writes in his *History of Sexuality* and *Sexual Morality and the Law* (1990) that the list of signatories included himself, Jean-Paul Sartre, Simone de Beauvoir, the jurist Jean Danet, filmmaker Alain Robbe-Grillet, writer Philippe Sollers, pediatrician and child psychoanalyst Françoise Dolto and many others holding political positions in the French government. In the Liberation paper in March 1979 another letter of petition signed by 63 intellectuals was published in support of a man who had fornicated with six to twelve year olds. It was asserted in the letter that a girl of six years old could give informed consent to sex with an adult. Refer to *Le Monde* (26th January 1977) and *Le devoir d'inventaire* by Remy Jacqueline (1st March 2001) in the online archives of the *L'Express* newspaper in a section titled *Libération Sexuelle* (Sexual Liberation). Contrary to *sexual liberation movements* desiring to legalize exploitation and fornication, Islām enjoins marriage and requires the consent of both the bride *and* the legal guardian as conditions for the legality of the marriage and to ensure the bride's welfare and protection. At the same time, Islām strictly outlaws grooming, fornication and infidelity.

Muslims are the First and Greatest Victims of the Khārijite Terrorists

As has become clear, the Prophet of Islām, Muḥammad (ﷺ) prophesized an extremist renegade group comprising of youthful and foolish, ignorant individuals who would depart from Islām, excommunicate Muslims and embark upon killing them. They appeared only 26 years later from the direction of Irāq and began slaughtering the Prophet's Companions after excommunicating them. They are known to the Muslim nation as the Khārijites, *extremist renegades.* Their primary targets are not non-Muslims, but Muslims whom they consider to be apostates because they disagree with their alien-to-Islām extremist views. The slaughter and annihilation of Muslims as a means of gaining wealth, leadership and power is their ultimate goal. The reason non-Muslims are targeted in the modern era and why terrorism exists in Western lands at all is because - *in the perception and view of the Khārijites* - the governments and armies of non-Muslims are meddling in Muslim lands and this hinders their goal of slaughtering Muslims and their leaders through violence, discord and revolution in order to acquire leadership, wealth and power. This is justified with the deceptive slogan of "*establishing the Khilāfah*" and "*establishing Islāmic Sharīʿah.*"

These people did not appear in 1993, 1995, or 2001. They appeared almost 1400 years ago in the year 657CE (26H). They are motivated by wealth, land and power and not religion because the Qurʾān does not go beyond their throats. This is what the Prophet Muḥammad (ﷺ) said about them in numerous famous and authentic traditions which are common knowledge to the Scholars of the Muslims, their students and many of the common-folk, "*They are the most evil of the creation*" and he stated, "*Each time they appear, they will be cut off until the Dajjāl (Anti-Christ) will appear in the midst of their armies*" and "*If I was to reach them, I would slaughter them, like the slaughtering of ʿĀd (a destroyed nation of the past)*" meaning, every last one of them until none of them remain, and "*They are the Dogs of*

Hellfire" and, "*Wherever you meet them, kill them, for there is a reward on the Day of Judgement for whoever kills them*" and "*They are the worst of those killed beneath the canopy of the sky.*"

The Khārijites are resentful that they have been hindered from the greater, primary goal of cleansing Muslim lands of "apostate" rulers and subjects. This ideology is present and detailed in the works of **Sayyid Quṭb**, their modern ideological grandfather. Western foreign policy is not the cause of the existence of these extremists.[159] It is an evil ideology *diametrically opposed* to everything Islām stands for and it appeared at the very dawn of Islām in a people motivated by other than Islām but acting upon the pretence that it is Islām. In the past 1400 years, since 657CE (26H) exponentially more Muslims have been killed by these extremists and their terrorism than non-Muslims in the past 20 years. And in the past 20 years, exponentially more Muslims have been killed by these brutal savages than non-Muslims. In Algeria alone, during ten years from 1991, there were almost 200,000 Muslim deaths due primarily *because* of the appearance of the takfīrī ideology whose enmity is towards Islām and its people before anyone else. So to mock the Prophet of Islām (صَلَّى ٱللَّٰهُ عَلَيْهِ وَسَلَّمَ) and ascribe the actions of these people to him and his message **is motivated first by pure ignorance and if it is not ignorance, then ideological hate**. In that case, it is not motivated by "*freedom of speech*" - which is merely an excuse for spreading hate propaganda.

In a 2009 report by the Combating Terrorism Center titled "*Deadly Vanguards: A Study of al-Qaʿida's Violence Against Muslims,*" authors Scott Helfstein, Nassir Abdullāh and Muḥammd al-Obaidi established,

[159] This is a fallacious claim often used by terrorist sympathizers to justify or explain away the atrocities committed by these evil people. They also use the errors, sins and lifestyles of rulers and the presence of social inequality in Muslim lands as *an explanatory excuse* for the emergence of Khārijite ideology, thereby intending to say, "It's not their fault, the circumstances forced them to react in this way." This is an evil narrative and is propounded by ignoramuses who do not value the Prophetic traditions and the judgements made therein upon the likes of these people.

through a solid research methodology, that al-Qāʿidah kills eight times more Muslims than non-Muslims, and even more when the division is expanded into *Western* and *non-Western* victims. Der Spiegel published a review of the report on 3rd December 2009, a summarization of which is presented: [160] "*Surprising Study On Terrorism: Al-Qaida Kills Eight Times More Muslims Than Non-Muslims.* Few would deny that Muslims too are victims of Islamist terror. But a new study by the Combating Terrorism Center in the US has shown that an overwhelming majority of al-Qaida victims are, in fact, co-religionists. *New Report Shows Many More Muslims Killed Than Non-Muslims.* It is, of course, no surprise that al-Qaida kills more Muslims than non-Muslims - particularly for people in the Islamic world. But a new report by the Combating Terrorism Center (CTC) at the United States' Military Academy at West Point in New York which has gathered together these and other relevant figures in one report '*Deadly Vanguards: A Study Of al-Qaida's Violence Against Muslims,*' spells out the discrepancy in black and white. *Non-Westerners 38 Times More Likely To Be Killed.* Put another way, between 2006 and 2008, non-Westerners were 38 times more likely to be killed by an al-Qaida attack than Westerners." End of quote.

The Washington Times also covered the report on 14th January 2010 in an editorial, an excerpt of which are provided: "Muslims are the main victims of al Qaeda's deadly terrorist attacks against the West, despite claims by the group's leaders that only a few Muslims have died in the organization's global war against Westerners, according to a study by the Combating Terrorism Center at West Point, N.Y. In 2007, al Qaeda's second in command, Ayman al-Zawahri said in a document he wrote called the 'The Power of Truth' that 'we haven't killed the innocents; not in Baghdad, nor in Morocco, nor in Algeria, nor anywhere else. And if there is any innocent who was killed in the mujahedeen's operations, then it was either an unintentional error, or out of necessity.' The report, published in December by Scott

[160] Refer to http://www.spiegel.de and it can be found via online search.

Helfstein, Nassar Abdullah and Mohammad al-Obaidi, scholars at the U.S. Military Academy at West Point center, concluded that al Qaeda has done just the opposite and that the group's terrorist actions from 2004 to 2008 led to more non-Western deaths than Western killings and have turned many of Islam's faithful against the extremist group. 'The fact is that the vast majority of al Qaeda's victims are Muslims: The analysis here shows that only 15 percent of the fatalities resulting from al Qaeda attacks between 2004 and 2008 were Westerners,' according to the report, titled 'Deadly Vanguards: A Study of Al Qaeda's Violence Against Muslims.' 'Many victims of al Qaeda and its affiliates have been Muslim, and people in the Muslim world know that. This explains why many Muslims deplore al Qaeda, and why you see more Muslim voices these days expressing strong opposition to al Qaeda and the ideology it espouses,' the report states. 'Despite numerous warnings and ongoing public debates about the indiscriminate use of violence, al Qaeda remains committed to its current tactics as displayed by the steady stream of Muslim fatalities from 2006 to 2008.' The study, which focused on al Qaeda violence from 2004 to 2008, stated that only 15 percent of the 3,010 victims killed in al Qaeda-related attacks were Western. The research also found that during the period from 2006 to 2008, only 2 percent (12 of 661 victims) were from the West, and the remaining 98 percent of those killed were inhabitants of countries with Muslim majorities. 'During this period, a person of non-Western origin was 54 times more likely to die in an al Qaeda attack than an individual from the West,' the report states. 'The overwhelming majority of al Qaeda victims are Muslims living in Muslim countries, and many are citizens of Iraq, which suffered more al Qaeda attacks than any other country courtesy of the al Qaeda in Iraq (AQI) affiliate.' The researchers of the study used 'Arabic media sources to study the victims of al Qaeda's violence through a nonprism.' Researchers said it was to 'avoid accusations of bias associated with Western news outlets or U.S. datasets.' 'Al Qaeda and sympathizers consistently argue that Western media outlets are no more than propaganda machines, and therefore, any reports or data they release distort facts or lack accuracy,' the researchers said. The recent killings of seven CIA officers in Afghanistan's eastern province of Khost by Jordanian-born bomber and double agent Humam Khalil Abu-Mulal al-Balawi was the most significant al Qaeda attack on a Western group this year. However, overall, U.S. intelligence officials agree with the report's findings that al Qaeda attacks have taken many more Muslim lives than those they target. 'Many victims of al Qaeda and its affiliates have been Muslim, and people in the Muslim world know that,' a U.S. counterterrorism official told The Washington Times." End quote.

It is no longer disputed that Muslims are the greatest of victims of terrorism perpetrated in the name of Islām. To well-informed Muslims, this is not news. This is because from the prominent traits mentioned by the Prophet Muḥammad (ﷺ) which belong to the Khārijite terrorists is that they kill the people of Islām and leave alone those besides them.[161] Terrorist incidents in the West that involve Muslims as perpetrators receive focused and sustained news coverage whereas those in which Muslims are the victims in various parts of the world do not receive the same attention. This naturally creates the perception that terrorism performed in the name of Islām is directed primarily and only towards non-Muslims. That is far from the truth on ideological grounds as has preceded in our discussion of the Khārijite ideology and also on practical grounds. This leads us to another set of statistics regarding the percentage of terrorist incidents involving Muslims in the lands of Europe.

---

[161] These traditions can be found in the collections of al-Bukhārī and Muslim. Terrorism in Western lands is merely a by-product, not something primarily intended by the Khārijites. Their primary targets are Muslim governments and their subjects. Imām al-Ājurrī (d. 360H, 10th century CE), said, "The scholars, past and present have not differed in that the Khārijites are an evil people, disobedient to Allāh the Exalted and His Messenger (ﷺ), even if they pray, fast and strive in worship. They claim to enjoin the good and prohibit the evil, but that will not benefit them... The Khārijites are evil, impure and vile, as are all the [variant] factions of Khārijites who are upon their doctrine...they revolt against the rulers and make lawful the killing of Muslims." In his excellent book titled, *al-Sharīʿah* (1/136).

Muslims in Regional and Global Terrorism

Europol publishes an annual report titled *Terrorism Situtation and Trend Report* and so far has eight editions.[162] In each report a table is presented of terrorist attacks in European countries based upon the type of terrorism. Five categories exist: Islamist, Separatist, Left-Wing, Right-Wing and Other. The following table charts total terrorist attacks by type. In some years, the figures include failed, foiled and successfully executed attacks.

	Islamist	Separatist	Left-Wing	Right-Wing	Other
2006	1	424	55	1	17
2007	4	532	21	1	24
2008	0	397	28	0	11
2009	1	237	40	4	10
2010	3	160	45	0	40
2011	0	110	37	1	26
2012	6	167	18	2	26
2013	0	84	24	0	44
Total	**15**	**2411**	**268**	**9**	**198**

Note: In the 2012 figures, the *Islamist* column was changed to *Religiously inspired.*

From the above table we can see that 99.48% of terrorist incidents (about 199 out of 200) were not by those referred to as *Islamists.* Putting it the other way around, 0.52% (around 1 in 200) of all terrorist acts in Europe were by *Islamists.*[163] In 2005 a total of 52 deaths

[162] The reports can be downloaded from europol.eu.

[163] The term "*Islamists*" is out of place and unwarranted in light of the many Prophetic traditions mentioned in this book. The more befitting term is "*Khārijite renegades.*" In fact, in the view of numerous scholarly authorities past and present it ought to be "*Apostates*" if these attacks were inspired and

resulted from the 7/7 attacks in London, UK, but between 2006 and 2010 the Europol reports show zero deaths arising from a total of nine attacks attributed to *Islamists* indicating the sporadic nature of these attacks. A report by Mother Jones, an investigative American political analysis magazine, indicates that out of roughly three million Muslims living in the United States, 0.007% (210) have been charged in domestic terror plots.[164] The picture which emerges from the data is that although horrendous attacks take place in the West from time to time with some having a significant number of casualties, there are more frequent, equally horrendous, large-scale terrorist attacks against Muslims which are justified through the same anti-Islāmic Khārijite, terrorist ideology. An example is the recent slaughter of 141 schoolchildren in Peshawar by the Taliban[165] and others which do not receive the same level of media coverage. Statistics indicate that terrorist attacks with most combined fatalities overall take place in Africa, Asia and the Middle East and whilst most terrorist attacks are masked with the "*Islamist*" label, the true underlying motives are political or economical in nature and not religious, even if deceptive religious rhetoric is employed to mask such motives.

In the next section we take a look at the subject of jihād and dispel common misconceptions employed by both Islam-hating loons and Khārijite terrorist savages in disfiguring the picture of Islām.

---

motivated by the ideology of the Khārijites in which the unlawful in the Islāmic Sharīʿah (taking innocent life) is declared to be lawful.

[164] Many of these plots are cases involving entrapment in which intelligence agents pretend to be extremists. Gullible, emotionally-led, ignorant Muslims are recruited in mosques, then cultivated and convinced to partake in a terrorist plot. At the appropriate crucial point, a sting operation concludes the entire episode and the foiling of an alleged terrorist plot is announced on major news channels. Refer to, "*The Informants*" by Trevor Aaronson in the September 2011 issue of Mother Jones magazine (available online). You can also search for "Muslim entrapment" and similar keywords. Refer also Stephen Down and Kathy Manley's detailed 178-page academic study titled, "*Inventing Terrorists: The Lawfare of Preemptive Prosecution.*"

[165] *Pakistan Taliban: Peshawar school attack leaves 141 dead*, BBC 16th December 2014.

The Prophet of Islām and Jihād

Jihād means *to engage in struggle* and comprises many forms. From its numerous outward manifestations is the jihād of fighting (*qitāl*) whose objective is to remove hindrance from the peaceful proclamation and practice of Islām, to protect its adherents from oppression and tribulation and to establish justice. That which is done by al-Qāʿidah, ISIS, the Ṭālibān and Boko Ḥarām is not jihād but corruption motivated by political, social and economic factors. It has no connection to the teachings of Islām, even if it is clothed in the garment of Islām and made to appear as such.

The famous Islāmic scholar, Ibn al-Qayyim (d. 751H 13th century CE) said: "And when Allāh sent His Messenger (صَلَّىٱللَّهُعَلَيْهِوَسَلَّمَ), the majority of the people of the [various] religions responded to him and to his successors (caliphs) after him, willingly, out of choice. He did not compel a single person to [accept] the religion, ever. Rather, he would fight whoever waged war against him and fought against him. But as for the one who was peaceful with him or made a truce with him, he did not fight him and did not compel him to enter into his religion - fulfilling the command of His Lord - the Sublime - when he said, **'There is no compulsion in religion truth has become clear from falsehood'** (2:156). And this is a [statement of] negation with the meaning of *prohibition*, meaning "Do not compel anyone upon religion." This verse was revealed regarding some men amongst the Companions (of the Prophet). They had children who had become Jews and Christians prior to Islām. When Islām came, their fathers accepted Islām and they desired to compel their children upon the religion. So they were prohibited from that by Allāh - the Sublime so that they themselves could [willingly] choose to enter into Islām. That which is correct [regarding this verse] is that upon its generality of meaning, it applies to every non-Muslim... **It will become clear to whoever reflects upon the biographical account of the Prophet (صَلَّىٱللَّهُعَلَيْهِوَسَلَّمَ) that he did not compel a single person to accept his religion, ever.** Rather, he fought whoever fought against him (first). As for the one who made a truce with him, he never fought him so long as he remained upon the truce and did not violate his covenant. Rather, Allāh the Exalted commanded him to fulfil the covenant with them, so long as they abided by it, just as He, the Exalted said, **'So as long as they are upright toward you, be upright toward them'** (9:7). When he came to al-Madīnah he made peace treaties with the Jews and affirmed them upon their religion.[166] When they waged war against him and broke the covenant and initiated fighting against him, then he fought against them. Thereafter he showed favour to some of them (sparing them), banished others and killed others. Likewise when he made a truce with the Quraysh for ten years, he never initiated fighting against them until they initiated fighting against him and violated their covenant. When they did that, he fought against them in their lands. Prior to that, they had fought against him, such as when they desired (to kill) him on the day of Uḥud and the day of al-Khandaq and the day of Badr as well. They came to fight against him (first), but if they had turned away from him (and left him) he would not have fought them. **The intent here is that he (ﷺ) never compelled anyone to enter his religion, ever**. Rather, the people entered his religion wilfully, out of choice. The majority of the people of the Earth entered his call when guidance became clear to them and that He is the Messenger of Allāh in truth."[167] End quote.

THE INJUNCTIONS PERTAINING TO FIGHTING AND JIHĀD

An accurate chronological correlation of the verses of jihād with the history of the call of the Prophet Muḥammad (ﷺ) will repel many of the doubts regarding jihād. At the outset it must be made clear that war in the Islāmic Sharīʿah is not a war of colonialism or a war of economies or to dispossess people of their land, property and wealth or to globalize trade or open up "free markets" or to display the superiority of one's tribe, race or nation. Allāh (عَزَّوَجَلَّ) said, **"That**

[166] Meaning, that he did not force them to accept Islām, but made treaties and covenants with them which he honoured.
[167] *Ḥidāyat al-Hayārā* (Dār ʿĀlam al-Fawāʾid, pp. 29-30).

home of the Hereafter We assign to those who do not desire exaltedness upon the earth or corruption. And the [best] outcome is for the righteous." (28:83). Pursuing highness in authority and causing corruption on Earth is prohibited and is the way of tyrants. Rather, jihād was legislated to allow the instrument of peaceful preaching to take its course and to protect those who peacefully invite to Islām and to truth, justice, lofty morals and noble manners. It was legislated in order to remove tribulation (*fitnah*) and oppression (*ẓulm*). In the face of harm and transgression at the hands of the polytheists, the Prophet (صَلَّى ٱللَّٰهُ عَلَيْهِ وَسَلَّمَ) was initially commanded with patience, restraint and not to raise his hand in violence, "**Follow, [O Muḥammad], what has been revealed to you from your Lord - there is no deity except Him - and turn away from those who associate others with Allah.**" (6:106) and "**So turn aside from them and say, 'Peace.' But they will come to know.**" (43:89).

But the hostitilies never ceased and attempts to kill the Prophet (صَلَّى ٱللَّٰهُ عَلَيْهِ وَسَلَّمَ) and his followers increased even after they had migrated to al-Madīnah to escape persecution. Permission was then granted to fight in the second stage, "**Permission [to fight] has been given to those who are being fought against, because they were wronged. And indeed, Allāh is competent to give them victory.**" (22:39). In this stage Muslims were not obligated to fight against the transgressors and oppressors, but merely *permitted* to defend themselves.

In the third stage, Muslims were obligated to fight against the transgressors who initiated fighting and caused injury and death, "**Fight in the way of Allāh those who fight you but do not transgress. Indeed. Allāh does not like transgressors.**" (2:190). In this fighting Muslims were cautioned against oppression even when repelling oppression from themselves just as they were commanded to cease fighting if the hostilities ceased and to make peace if it was offered, "**So if they remove themselves from you and do not fight you and offer you peace, then Allāh has not made for you a cause [for fighting] against them.**" (4:90) If the transgressing enemy did not withdraw, cease hostilities and offer peace, they were to be pursued and fought against, "**If they withdraw not from you, nor offer you peace, nor restrain their hands, take (hold) of them and kill them wherever you find them. In their case, We have provided you with a clear warrant against them.**" (4:91). Fighting and killing those who did not cease their hostilities after they were fought against to repel their initial transgression is warranted and justified in this verse.

Yet in all instances, going beyond the limits in fighting was prohibited, "**So whoever has assaulted you, then assault him *in the same way* that he has assaulted you. And fear Allah and know that Allah is with those who fear Him.**" (2:194). Further, Muslims were commanded to make only a proportionate response whilst being mindful and fearful of Allāh by not transgressing beyond the bounds. And in another verse, "**And expel them from wherever they have expelled you and fitnah (tribulation)[168] is worse than killing.**" (2:191). Further, the revelation made it clear that if the transgressing party inclines towards peace, the Muslims are also to incline towards peace, "**And if they incline to peace, then incline to it [also] and rely upon Allāh. Indeed, it is He who is the Hearing, the Knowing.**" (8:61).

The objectives behind this obligatory fighting are stated in the Qur'ān, "**And what is [the matter] with you that you fight not in the cause of Allāh and [for] the oppressed among men, women, and children who say, 'Our Lord, take us out of this city of oppressive people and appoint for us from Yourself a protector and appoint for us from Yourself a helper?'**" (4:75). In other words, this fighting was enjoined in aid of the oppressed men, women and children whose people violently transgressed against them for no fault on their behalf save their faith in just one Lord and worshipping Him alone exclusive to

[168] The fitnah in this verse refers to a Muslim being victimized, oppressed or killed because of his practice of Islām. This was the behaviour of the polytheists whenever they came to learn that a person had become a Muslim. This type of tribulation is more severe than the act of fighting against them to end their tribulation and oppression.

other deities. In another verse, there occurs, "**Fight them until there is no more tribulation (fitnah)**[169] **and [until] worship is [acknowledged to be] for Allāh. But if they cease, then there is to be no aggression except against the oppressors.**"(2:193). The fighting in this verse was enjoined due to the fighting that had been initiated by the polytheists to put Muslims to trial without just cause. It also commanded that should their oppression cease, Muslims should cease fighting in response. The underlying reason for the legislation of this fighting was to remove tribulation (*fitnah*) and to allow worship to be acknowledged for Allāh (عَزَّوَجَلَّ).

Further, throughout these periods of war, treaties and covenants were to be honoured. Coming to the aid of the oppressed and weak through fighting was made conditional upon the absence of existing treaties and covenants with the aggressing non-Muslims, "**Indeed, those who have believed and emigrated and fought with their wealth and lives in the cause of Allāh and those who gave shelter and aided - they are allies of one another. But those who believed and did not emigrate - for you there is no guardianship of them until they emigrate. And if they seek help of you for the religion, then you must help, except against a people between yourselves and whom is a treaty. And Allāh is Seeing of what you do.**" (8:72). This verse makes reference to the emigrants (muhājirūn) who left Makkah for al-Madīnah because it was hostile and dangerous. Those who received them, gave them shelter and aid were the helpers (anṣār). As for those Muslims who remained in Makkah, the Muslims in al-Madinah had no responsibility of guardianship over them unless they emigrated. And if those Muslims in Makkah sought aid from the Muslims in al-Madīnah against the transgressing party, the Muslims were obliged to aid them unless

[169] The non-Muslims and polytheists did not fight the Muslims except to put them to trial and make them leave their religion. Thus, the meaning of "**And fight them until there is no more tribulation and worship is acknowledged to be for Allāh**"(2:193) is: Until aggression and hindrance is repelled so that the Muslims are no longer put to trial in their religion and are free to proclaim it so that worship can be for Allāh alone.

there was a treaty between them and the transgressing party. This indicates the great regard in Islām for treaties and covenants even when their terms are unfavourable. Violating covenants and treaties is from the traits of the hypocrites and does not reconcile with faith.

However, when the aggressive parties showed no restraint in their hostilities and desired to kill the Prophet (صَلَّى ٱللَّهُ عَلَيْهِ وَسَلَّمَ) and wipe out his community in al-Madīnah[170] and made clear this was an objective they would continue to pursue even by violating treaties, disassociation was made from these treaties because the aggressors had taken them as advantageous means to continue pursuing their hostile agendas. Allāh (عَزَّوَجَلَّ) revealed, "**[A declaration of] disassociation, from Allāh and His Messenger, to those with whom you had made a treaty among the polytheists.**" (9:1) An exception was made for those who had honoured their treaties, "**Excepted are those with whom you made a treaty among the polytheists and then they have not been deficient toward you in anything or supported anyone against you; so complete for them their treaty until their term [has ended]. Indeed, Allāh loves the righteous [who fear Him].**" (9:4). And also a little later, "**Except those with whom you made a treaty at the [sacred precincts] of the mosque. So long as they are upright with you, be upright with them. Indeed, Allah loves the righteous [who fear Him].**"(9:7). Once more, we see the emphasis on being truthful in covenants and treaties and fulfilling them, this being a trait of the righteous whom Allāh loves. These treaties were to be honoured by Muslims until their term of duration expired. Thereafter, when all treaties had been annulled the treacherous enemies were to be sought wherever they were found, "**And when the sacred months have passed, then kill the polytheists wherever you find them and capture them and besiege them and sit in wait for them at every place of ambush. But if they should repent, establish prayer, and give zakāh, let them [go] on their way. Indeed,**

[170] This included actions of treachery and perfidy by some of those who were under covenant in al-Madīnah. They violated their treaties after ratifying them, demonstrating that they were not to be trusted and that they intended corruption and mischief, not peace.

Allah is Forgiving and Merciful." (9:5). And a little later, "**Would you not fight a people who broke their oaths and determined to expel the Messenger, and they had begun [the attack upon] you the first time?**" (9:13). In this stage, the Prophet (صَلَّى ٱللَّٰهُ عَلَيْهِ وَسَلَّمَ) was commanded to make jihād against the enemy with whom there was no peace treaty (*ṣulḥ*), covenant (*āhd*), security (*amān*) or guarantee (*dhimmāh*) in order to remove hindrance from the proclamation and practice of Islām and to ensure no one was prevented from hearing its message peacefully.[171] Looking at these verses in their proper historical context reveals the restraint, mercy and justice with which the Prophet (صَلَّى ٱللَّٰهُ عَلَيْهِ وَسَلَّمَ) was commanded even in matters of fighting and war.

NON-COMBATANTS ARE NOT TO BE KILLED

Muslim scholars have discussed the basis upon which fighting against non-Muslims has been warranted.[172] Disbelief (*kufr*) is not the unique, independent factor which warrants fighting.[173] Ibn Taymiyyah said, "As for those who do not cause hindrance and engage in fighting such as women, children, ascetics, the old, the blind, the chronically ill and their likes, they are not to be killed in the view of the majority of the scholars... fighting is for the one who fights against us when we desire to proclaim the religion of Allāh."[174] He also said, "As for the disbeliever, it is permissible to enter into a security or truce arrangement with him and as for the captive, he can be freed or used as ransom. And if he is from the People of the Book it is permitted to offer him a guarantee of protection (*dhimmah*) and for their food to be

---

171 It is agreed upon by all Muslim scholars that this jihād is performed solely by and at the discretion of a ruler of a legitimate Islamic government after his determination that such a measure will be in the interests of his state and will lead to justice being established. It is not for the insurgents, renegades or terrorists whose evil, destructive actions have no connection to jihād at all.

172 In other words is the command to fight a people merely *because* they are disbelievers or is it because of the presence of other factors.

173 Had the cause of fighting been disbelief (*kufr*) alone, killling women, children, the elderly, priests and monks would not have been prohibited.

174 *Majmūʿ al-Fatāwā* (8/354).

consumed and their women to be married. Their women are not to be killed unless they directly engage in fighting through speech or deed by agreement of all the scholars. Likewise, those who do not engage in fighting amongst them are not to be killed in the view of the majority of the scholars, as has been indicated in the Sunnah (Prophetic tradition)."[175]

As for the claim that the verses pertaining to jihād abrogated the verses which enjoin peaceful preaching with benevolence, wisdom and patience and the verses which command just dealing with those who do not fight the Muslims then this is incorrect. One can refer to Imām al-Shanqītī's discussion in the next section and also to Ibn Taymiyyah's discussion of this matter in *al-Jawāb al-Ṣaḥīḥ* in which he explains that the verse pertaining to inviting to Islām with wisdom, beautiful admonition and good argument[176] is a decisive (*muḥkam*) verse which has not been abrogated by any verse at all. He proceeds to provide numerous angles of evidence to establish this and explains that both approaches of peace and war are legislated and may be resorted to by a Muslim ruler and his government depending on the circumstances.[177] Finally, it is also from jihād in the path of Allāh (عَزَّوَجَلَّ) for a Muslim ruler to fight the Khārijite terrorists.[178] This now leads us to the discussion of Muslim relations with those non-Muslims who do not fight against the Muslims on account of their religion.

---

175 *Majmūʿ al-Fatāwā* (8/414).

176 Allāh (عَزَّوَجَلَّ) said, "**Invite to the way of your Lord with wisdom and good instruction, and argue with them in a way that is best. Indeed, your Lord is most knowing of who has strayed from His way, and He is most knowing of who is [rightly] guided.**" (16:125).

177 Refer to *al-Jawāb al-Ṣaḥīḥ* (1/217). All injunctions pertaining to jihād in the Islāmic texts are under the operation and supervision of the ruler.

178 Shaykh Muḥammad bin ʿAbd al-Wahhāb (رَحِمَهُ ٱللَّهُ) said, "As for the people of [deviant] innovations such as the Khārijites, they desire to corrupt the religion of the people." *Masāʾīl Lakhkhaṣahā al-Imām* in his *Majmuʿ Muʾallafāt* (2/2/90). The Prophet (ﷺ) ordered that they be fought against as is manifest in his traditions. Repelling the deviant innovators who corrupt Islām and harm its people is from the types and levels of jihād.

Muslim And Non-Muslim Relations

The Qur'ān has outlined the base rule concerning the relationship between Muslims and non-Muslims who do not fight the Muslims on account of their religion and nor expel Muslims from their homes. Allāh (سُبْحَانَهُ وَتَعَالَىٰ) stated in Sūrah al-Mumtahinah:

لَّا يَنْهَىٰكُمُ ٱللَّهُ عَنِ ٱلَّذِينَ لَمْ يُقَٰتِلُوكُمْ فِى ٱلدِّينِ وَلَمْ يُخْرِجُوكُم مِّن دِيَٰرِكُمْ أَن تَبَرُّوهُمْ
وَتُقْسِطُوٓا۟ إِلَيْهِمْ ۚ إِنَّ ٱللَّهَ يُحِبُّ ٱلْمُقْسِطِينَ ﴿٨﴾

> **Allāh does not forbid you from those who do not fight you because of religion and do not expel you from your homes - from being righteous toward them and acting justly toward them. Indeed, Allāh loves those who act justly.** (60:8).

The classical commentator and Salafī scholar, **Ibn Kathīr** (رَحِمَهُ ٱللَّٰهُ) stated in his exegesis of this verse, "Meaning, that you are benevolent towards them and deal justly with them"[179] and **Imām 'Abd al-Raḥmān bin Nāṣir al-Sa'dī** (رَحِمَهُ ٱللَّٰهُ), a Salafī scholar of the modern era stated in his exegesis of this verse, "Meaning: Allāh does not prohibit you from benevolent conduct, good ties, returning goodness and behaving with justice towards the polytheists, from those who are relatives and other than them, where they do not fight you for your religion and nor expel you from your homes."[180]

Ibn Kathir brings a number of narrations from Asmā' (رَضِيَ ٱللَّٰهُ عَنْهَا), the daughter of Abū Bakr (رَضِيَ ٱللَّٰهُ عَنْهُ), whose pagan mother came to visit her in al-Madīnah, explaining that this was the reason for the revelation of this particular verse. Asmā' said, "My mother who was a pagan approached (al-Madīnah) during the truce with (the tribe of) Quraysh, so I came to the Prophet (صَلَّى ٱللَّٰهُ عَلَيْهِ وَسَلَّمَ) and said, 'O Messenger of Allāh, my

[179] Refer to his *Tafsīr al-Qur'ān al-Aẓīm* under the explanation of this verse.
[180] Refer to *Taysīr al-Karīm al-Raḥmān*.

mother has come and she desires to see me, shall I keep ties with her?' He said, 'Yes, keep the ties of kinship with your mother'."[181]

Ibn Jarīr al-Ṭabarī (رَحِمَهُ ٱللَّه), another classical Salafī commentator explains in his exegesis that there were a number of opinions regarding this particular verse, and mentions amongst them: First, that this verse was particular only to those Muslims who were residing in Makkah but had not yet emigrated to al-Madīnah. Second, that this verse relates to people outside of Makkah who had not emigrated to al-Madīnah. Third, that this verse was regarding the pagans of Makkah who did not fight the Muslims nor expel them from their homes, but that it was later abrogated with the command to fight the pagans on account of their violation of the truce. Then al-Ṭabari explains the correct viewpoint, stating therein, "The most correct of these sayings is the statement of the one who said that what is meant by, **"Allāh does not forbid you to deal justly and kindly with those who fought not against you on account of religion"** (is that it pertains to) all of the factions from the varying beliefs and religions. That you behave good towards them, and that you are just regarding them, because Allāh (عَزَّوَجَلَّ) generalised with His saying, **"...those who fought not against you on account of your religion and did not drive you out of your homes."** So this applies to everyone who is characterized by this. He did not specify some as opposed to others in this regard." End quote. And then al-Ṭabarī goes on to discredit the view of those who said this injunction was abrogated.[182]

The esteemed Salafī Scholar of the 20th century **Muḥammad Amīn al-Shanqīṭī** (رَحِمَهُ ٱللَّه), has a lengthy discussion in his exegesis, *Aḍwā' al-Bayān* (6/146 onwards). He mentions the numerous views, including the viewpoint that this verse was abrogated and proceeds to provide historical and textual evidences to discredit this view, mentioning: **One:** The statements of al-Ṭabarī and Imām al-Shāfiʿī, after which he

---

[181] Related by al-Bukhārī.
[182] Refer to *Jāmiʿ al-Bayān* (*Tafsīr al-Ṭabarī*) under this verse.

says said, "This (view) that has been deemed correct by Ibn Jarir (al-Ṭabarī) and which was authenticated by al-Shafi'ī (رحمه الله) is that which is necessitated by spirit of the Islamic legislation." **Two:** The benevolence of the Prophet (ﷺ) towards specific non-Muslims, such as Thumāmā who had come to assassinate the Prophet but was captured by the Muslims. He was treated well, eventually released and he voluntarily became a Muslim. **Three:** The various delegations that came to the Prophet (ﷺ) in the 9th year after the hijra. Such as the Christians of Najrān, and the delegation of Tamīm, and others. With all of them, the Prophet (ﷺ) was gentle and kind, he was benevolent towards them. **Four:** The treatment of the Jews of Khaybar who despite being treacherous, scheming a variety of intrigues, inciting the Banī Quraydhah and plotting against the Prophet (ﷺ) on numerous occasions, were spared. After being forced to surrender they were allowed to live off their land whilst giving a share of the produce to the Muslims. **Five:** The verse in the Qur'ān regarding the treatment of non-Muslim parents who force a person to worship others besides Allāh. Al-Shanqīṭī said, "And in closing, that which makes this clear very strongly, and about which no one has claimed abrogation is the saying of (Allāh), the Exalted, '**And if they both strive to make you associate with Me (in worship) that of which you have no knowledge, then do not obey them. But accompany them in this life with goodness.**' (31:15). This good behaviour and benevolence is towards the one who strove to make a Muslim associate others with Allāh (in worship) but did not actually fight against the Muslims. Hence, the right of the parents are to be given precedence, even if they are upon disbelief, and strive to lead one to associationism (shirk)."

With these and other evidences al-Shanqīṭī invalidates the view of those who spoke with abrogation of this verse. Al-Shanqīṭī covered this issue in some depth in his *Aḍwā' al-Bayān*, explaining, "And we have lengthened the speech regarding this matter due to its importance and the dire need for it today."

RELATIONSHIPS WITH JEWS AND CHRISTIANS

It is known from the biography of Prophet Muḥammad (صَلَّى ٱللَّهُ عَلَيْهِ وَسَلَّمَ) that he had relations with Jews and Christians even though their religion was abrogated with the revelation of the Qur'ān and although many of them believed in him, others remained upon their religion. The learned amongst them knew Muḥammad (صَلَّى ٱللَّهُ عَلَيْهِ وَسَلَّمَ) was mentioned in their scriptures. Many delegations of Christians would come to him to learn about Islām. From them were the delegations of Najrān whom he would graciously accommodate. Most of them became Muslims after discussions and debates with the Prophet (صَلَّى ٱللَّهُ عَلَيْهِ وَسَلَّمَ). In the constitution (dustūr) of al-Madīnah, the Prophet (صَلَّى ٱللَّهُ عَلَيْهِ وَسَلَّمَ) declared - affirming the Jews upon their faith, "For the Jews of Banū ʿAwf are one community with the Believers. To the Jews their religion and to the Muslims their religion, their leaders and themselves - except the one who oppresses and sins, for he only destroys himself and the people of his household. For the Jews of Banū al-Najjār is the same as what is for the Jews of Banū ʿAwf. For the Jews of Banū al-Ḥārith is the same as what is for the Jews of Banū ʿAwf. For the Jews of Banū Sāʿidah is the same as what is for the Jews of Banū ʿAwf. For the Jews of Banū Jashm is the same as what is for the Jews of Banū ʿAwf. For the Jews of Banū al-ʿAws is the same as what is for the Jews of Banū ʿAwf. And for the Jews of Banū Thaʿlabah is the same as what is for the Jews of Banū ʿAwf, save whoever transgresses and sins for he only destroys himself and the people of his household... and that the expenditure of the Jews is upon them and the expenditure of the Muslims is upon them."

In this constitution, the Prophet (صَلَّى ٱللَّهُ عَلَيْهِ وَسَلَّمَ) guaranteed security of life. No one was killed except the one who acted treacherously and violated the covenant by turning against the Muslims and allying with others to plot their murder and demise. He affirmed for the Jews their freedom to practice their religion, their right of ownership and right to trade. He guaranteed their defence and protection against external enemies. He also guaranteed justice in all dealings and removal of oppression if they were subject to it by others. When al-Ashʿat bin

Qays, a man from the Muslims, disputed with a man amongst the Jews regarding some land in Yemen and no clear proof was presented, the Prophet (ﷺ) judged in favour of the Jew.[183] In fact, he permitted the Jews to judge according to their own law in disputes between them and did not impose upon them in their own disputes unless they came and sought his judgement in a dispute.[184] The Prophet (ﷺ) behaved with justice, benevolence, good manners and fulfilment of trusts. From his good behaviour with the Jews in particular is that he would visit their sick as is related by Anas bin Mālik that a boy amongst the Jews who would serve the Prophet in his chores fell sick and he went to visit him and invited him to Islām. The boy's father ordered his son to obey the Prophet, indicating the reverence and respect which Jews had for the Prophet. The Jewish boy became a Muslim.[185] He would accept gifts from the Jews and also had trade dealings with the Jews. 'Ā'ishah (رَضِيَ اللَّهُ عَنْهَا) reported that the Prophet (ﷺ) purchased some food from a Jew on credit and mortgaged his iron shield for it.[186] The Jews would often pass by him and ask him questions on religious matters. On an occasion they asked him about the soul (rūḥ) as a result of which a verse in the Qur'an was revealed. He would also supplicate for them for guidance and rectification. Alongside this, the Prophet (ﷺ) meted out justice to anyone who acted treacherously or with treason, violated the covenants, disturbed the peace and worked mischief and corruption on earth.[187]

---

[183] The story is related in both al-Bukhārī and Muslim.

[184] The Islāmic Sharī'ah grants religious minorities the right to judge by their own laws indicating that it is fairer and more accommodating than secular laws in which everyone is obligated to abide by a law which they may or may not be in agreement with. In this regard, the Islāmic Sharī'ah is more tolerant of other faiths than secular constitutions and laws.

[185] Related by al-Bukhāri (no. 1356).

[186] Related by al-Bukhārī (no. 1990) and Muslim (no. 1603).

[187] Hence, those who resorted to treachery after ratifying their covenant and plotted with outside enemies to murder the Prophet (ﷺ) in order to put an end to the Muslim state were delivered justice. They were not wronged because they chose treachery with full knowledge of the outcome.

TRADE RELATIONS WITH PEACEFUL AND WARRING NATIONS

What illustrates the difference between genuine Islāmic scholarship and the compound ignorance or pretentiousness of the Khārijites is the fact that they treat dealings between Muslims and non-Muslims which are perfectly legal in the Islāmic Sharīʿah to be manifestations of disbelief (*kufr*). On the basis of such actions, they declare rulers and whole governments to be apostates against whom their twisted version of jihād is to be waged. Whilst the examples are numerous we can use just one issue to highlight the affair briefly and concisely. The Islāmic legislation permits **trade relations** even with an enemy that engages in war, let alone a people or a nation not engaged in war.[188]

Imām al-Shanqīṭī (رَحِمَهُ ٱللَّهُ) said, "That which al-Ṭabarī and al-Shāfiʿī deemed correct is something necessitated by the spirit of the Islāmic legislation. As for the angle from which we promised to present, then it is that the Muslims today have shared interests with each other and these interests are tied to all the nation states of the world whether those of the polytheists or the People of the Book. It is not possible for the ummah today to live in isolation from the rest of the nation states due to the interdependent, intertwined nature of their beneficial interests. This is especially so in the field of economy. Life would become difficult in terms of (essential) products, manufacturing and trade markets. In light of this, the verse grants support to the permissibility of interactions and exchanging beneficial interests with those who are peaceful on the basis of what was said by Ibn Jarīr [al-Ṭabarī] and explained by al-Shāfiʿī."[189] The renowned scholar of Prophetic traditions, Imām al-Bukhārī brings a subject heading in his compilation, "*Chapter: Buying and Selling with the Polytheists and People of War.*" Beneath this chapter heading he relates a tradition through

[188] The Prophet (ﷺ) died whilst his shield was mortgaged to a Jew from whom he had bought thirty weights of measure of barley which he had taken to feed his family. Related by Aḥmad in the Musnad (5/137), al-Tirmidhī (no. 1214), Ibn Mājah (no. 2439) and others from Ibn ʿAbbās.

[189] *Aḍwāʾ al-Bayān* (6/155). Referring to the verse (60:8) mentioned earlier.

ʿAbd al-Raḥmān bin Abū Bakr who said that a group of them were with the Prophet (ﷺ) when a tall man came with a flock of sheep. The Prophet said to him, "Sale or a gift?" The man said, "No, for sale." So the Prophet (ﷺ) purchased a sheep from him.[190] Commentators upon the traditions, such as Ibn Ḥajar al-ʿAsqalānī point out that it is permitted to engage in trade relations with non-Muslims except in relation to goods that will be used specifically in matters of war. Ibn Taymiyyah mentioned, on the basis of numerous traditions in this field, "If a man was to travel to the land of war in order to purchase from there, it would be permitted in our view, as is indicated in the report of Abu Bakr (رَضِيَ اللَّهُ عَنْهُ) trading - during the lifetime of the Prophet (ﷺ) - in the land of Shām (Syria) whilst it was a land of war."[191] He also discusses the permissibility of Muslims trading with the Mongol Tartars so long as the items of trade do not involve what is unlawful in the Sharīʿah.[192] Al-Ḥasan al-Baṣrī related that Abū Musā (رَضِيَ اللَّهُ عَنْهُ) wrote to ʿUmar (رَضِيَ اللَّهُ عَنْهُ), the second caliph, informing him that when Muslim traders enter the land of war, a ten percent (in tax) is taken from them. So ʿUmar (رَضِيَ اللَّهُ عَنْهُ) wrote back to him and said, "Take from them the likes of that when they come to our lands, ten percent."[193] Despite this, the Khārijites excommunicate rulers, governments and their instruments such as the military and police, judging them all to be apostates because of their diplomatic and trade relations with non-Muslim nations. This indicates the severity of their ignorance and lack of understanding of basic principles in the Sharīʿah. From what has preceded we see an entirely different narrative from the one promulgated by both the **Khārijite terrorist** and the **spiteful, hate-filled Islamophobe** in all his varying flavours - whether that be the lying cartoonist, the hatemonger and hatemongress that hosts or appears on news channels or the puppet funded by groups specializing in right-wing hate-propaganda. The Prophet (ﷺ) is exonerated from their lies and distortions.

---

190 Related by al-Bukhārī (no. 2103).

191 *Iqtiḍā' Ṣirāṭ al-Mustaqīm*, Dār ʿĀlam al-Kutub (2/15).

192 Refer to *Majmūʿ al-Fatāwā* (29/275).

193 *Al-Sunan* of al-Bayhaqī in Kitāb al-Jizyah (no. 19283).

Obligations of Muslims in Non-Muslim Lands

As for Muslims who reside in non-Muslim lands such as Europe, Britain, the United States, Canada and elsewhere, the late scholar, **Shaykh Muḥammad bin Ṣāliḥ al-'Uthaymīn** (رَحِمَهُ ٱللَّهُ) advised a large gathering of Muslims in the city of Birmingham in July 2000: "Likewise I invite you to have respect for those people who have the right that they should be respected, those between whom there is an agreement (of protection) for you. For the land in which you are living is such that there is an agreement between you and them. If this were not the case they would have killed you or expelled you. So preserve this agreement, and do not prove treacherous to it, since treachery is a sign of the hypocrites, and it is not from the way of the Believers. And know that it is authentically reported from the Prophet that he said, "*Whoever kills one who is under an agreement of protection will not smell the fragrance of Paradise.*" Do not be fooled by those sayings of the foolish people, those who say "Those people are non-Muslims, so their wealth is lawful for us (to misappropriate or take by way of murder and killing)." For by Allāh, this is a lie. A lie about Allāh's religion, and a lie about Islāmic societies. We may not say that it is lawful to be treacherous towards people whom we have an agreement with. O my brothers. O youth. O Muslims. Be truthful in your buying and selling, and renting, and leasing, and in all mutual transactions. Because truthfulness is from the characteristics of the Believers, and Allāh, (تَبَارَكَ وَتَعَالَىٰ) has commanded truthfulness in His saying, "**O you who believe, fear and keep you duty to Allāh and be with the truthful**" (9:119). And the Prophet encouraged truthfulness and said, "*Adhere to truthfulness, because truthfulness leads to goodness, and goodness leads to Paradise. And a person will continue to be truthful, and strive to be truthful until he will be written down with Allāh as a truthful person.*" And he warned against falsehood, and said, "*Beware of falsehood, because falsehood leads to wickedness, and wickedness leads to the Fire. And a person will continue lying, and striving to lie until he is written down with Allāh as a great liar.*" O my brother Muslims. O youth. Be true in your sayings with your brothers, and with those non-Muslims whom you live along with - so that you will be inviters to the religion of Islām, by your actions and in reality. So how many people there are who first entered into Islām because of the behaviour and manners of the Muslims, and their truthfulness, and their being true in their dealings."[194]

The late scholar, **Shaykh Aḥmad bin Yaḥyā al-Najmī** said: "The Prophet (صَلَّىٰٱللَّهُعَلَيْهِوَسَلَّمَ) would prohibit perfidy and treachery and he would command with truthfulness, innocence and trustworthiness... As for what the terrorists do in this time when they wear bombs or they drive cards loaded with bombs and when they find a gathering of people they blow themselves up or the blow the car up, then this practice is built upon deception, Islām is far, far away from this and does not affirm it at all. What is being done now of suicide missions in Britain or other lands, they are planned and excecuted by the Takfīrī Khārijites, those whom the Messenger of Allāh (صَلَّىٰٱللَّهُعَلَيْهِوَسَلَّمَ) rebuked..." - the Shaykh proceeds to cite the very harsh Prophetic traditions regarding the Khārijites whose mention has been made previously and then continues - "... It is known from this that Islām is free and innocent from these chaotic, reckless actions. The perpetrators are to be denounced and their actions are to be rejected. But those who accuse the Salafīs who follow the Book of Allāh, the Sunnah of His Messenger (صَلَّىٰٱللَّهُعَلَيْهِوَسَلَّمَ) and proceed upon the way of the Companions, those who accuse them of bombings in Britain or elsewhere, which comprise the killing of souls, destruction of wealth, shedding of blood, instilling fear (terror) into the people and revolting against the state... it is the very ones who perform these actions who accuse the Salafīs of these evils. They desire to attribute these actions to others besides them. These people are from the organization of al-Qāʿidah, those who follow Usāmah bin Lādin, [Muḥammad] al-Misʿarī and Saʿd al-Faqīh and their likes who have been nurtured upon the books of the thinkers such as Sayyid Quṭb."[195]

---

[194] From a tele-link recording on 28th July 2000 at a conference organized by Salafī Publications (Maktabah Salafiyyah).

[195] In a dictated statement issued following the 2005 London 7/7 attacks.

And the scholar, **Shaykh Rabīʿ bin Hādī** stated: "From the greatest and most-distinguished qualities enjoined by Islām is the fulfilment of covenants and the fulfilment of contracts and promises, even with the non-Muslims. And from the traits of the believers is the absence of treachery. And there occurs in the story of al-Mughīrah bin Shuʿbah, whilst he was a polytheist, that he accompanied a group of polytheists on a journey to Syria and killed them, taking their wealth. When he came to the Prophet (ﷺ), intending to accept Islām, he offered the wealth to him and told him of the story. The Prophet (ﷺ) said, "*As for (your) Islām, we accept it, but as for the wealth, it is wealth taken by treachery and we do not have any need of it.*"[196] This is because this wealth arose through treachery and Islām does not permit treachery in any situation whatsoever. Thus treachery and betrayal is not permissible, neither with the non-Muslims nor other than them. Destruction and chaos through this way (of using treachery) is not permissible because innocent women and children are killed. The enemies rejoice with this because it disfigures the picture of Islām and its people and it is used against Islām. So they give a picture of Islām that is blacker than the picture of corrupt religions, and this is the fruit of the actions of those people [the terrorists] upon Islām and the Muslims. Hence, it is upon the Muslims to be the striking example in truthfulness, lofty manners, fulfilment of trusts and to remain far away from these attributes of treachery, perfidy, deception, lying and taking life which does not benefit Islām but harms Islām."[197]

The scholar, **Shaykh Muḥammad bin Hādī**, during his lecture dated 13th May 2014 in the city of the Prophet Muḥammad (ﷺ), al-Madīnah, exhorted the 200 or so mostly Western attendees to adhere to **truthfulness** (*ṣidq*) in their dealings, contracts, and agreements with non-Muslims. Likewise he enjoined **gentleness** (*rifq*) towards them as well as **humility** (*tawāḍuʿ*) and illustrated each trait through practical examples from the Prophet Muḥammad (ﷺ).

---

[196] Related by Abū Dāwūd (no. 2765) and declared ṣaḥīḥ by al-Albānī.

[197] Abridged, from the cassette "*Verdicts of the Scholars on Assassinations and Bombings*" Tasjīlāt Minhāj al-Sunnah, Riyāḍ.

Terrorism Is Not Jihād

That which is fraudulently claimed to be jihād by the Khārijite terrorists is not jihād. It is corruption, mischief and destruction. Terrorism involves the violation of every lofty and noble trait which Islām inculcates in an individual: Truthfulness, honesty, fulfilment of covenants and contracts and so on. It involves every vile trait that Islām has outlawed: Lying, deception, treachery, perfidy, violating contracts and covenants.

Over the past 30 years **the Salafī scholars** in particular have been at the forefront of refuting and exposing this twisted, evil, corrupt idea of jihād[198] whose ideological origins lie with the **Ṣūfī Ash'arīs** of Egypt and figureheads of the Muslim Brotherhood (al-Ikhwān):[199]

---

[198] The statements of these scholars such as Shaykh al-Albānī, Shaykh Ibn Bāz, Shaykh Ibn al-'Uthaymīn, Shaykh al-Fawzān, Shaykh Rabī bin Hādī, Shaykh Aḥmad al-Najmī and Shaykh Zayd al-Madkhalī (who wrote a famous book called "*Terrorism and its Effects Upon Individuals and Nations*" almost 20 years ago) are all well known. Another scholar, Shaykh 'Abd al-Muḥsin al-'Abbād authored, "*With Which Intellect or Religiosity is Bombing and Destruction Considered to be Jihād?*" A huge body of Salafī literature exists on this subject spanning over the past three decades. It is strange that despite this clear stance over the past three decades, rather over the past 1400 years, equivocation is made between the ideology of the Khārijite terrorists and the creed and methodology of the Salafīs. Many an ignorant or dishonest academic continues to make a career out of the preposterous lie that Salafiyyah equates to extremism and terrorism. Rather, the Salafīs who follow the creed and methodology of the Companions are the very first of enemies to the Khāriijte terrorists, just as the third and fourth Caliphs, 'Uthmān and 'Alī (رَضِيَ اللَّهُ عَنْهُمَا) and the Prophet's Companions (رَضِيَ اللَّهُ عَنْهُمْ) as a whole were the first of enemies to the Khārijites in their time.

[199] Contrary to the propaganda from the Islamophobes, ignorant academics, "terrorism" experts and many others who have a sectarian bias against the Salafī way, the ideology of terrorism does not lie in the works and teachings of Muḥammad bin 'Abd al-Wahhāb nor Ibn Taymiyyah. Rather, this ideology lies in the books of Sayyid Quṭb, a Ṣūfī Ash'arī whose influences came from Marxism and Leninism, the writings of Alexis Carrel (the French philosopher), Abū A'lā Mawdūdī (the Indo-Pak "Islamist") and the poison of

Ḥasan al-Bannā, founder of the Muslim Brotherhood (al-Ikhwān) and **Sayyid Quṭb**, the founder of all modern-day takfirī movements. Muṣtafā Ramaḍān published an article[200] comprising interviews with three former members of al-Ikhwān who all consider Ḥasan al-Bannā to be the founder of the doctrine of mass takfīr (excommunication) of the Muslim ummah and hold that the call and methodogy of al-Ikhwān was built upon that very foundation, even if it was not explicitly preached prior to the era of Sayyid Quṭb in the 50s and 60s. During the late 1940s, with the approval of Ḥasan al-Bannā, terrorist activities were perpetrated against civilians and politicians in Egypt.[201] This included detonating bombs in crowded civilian areas. Less than two decades later, the fully developed modern and twisted, corrupted idea of jihād found itself expressed in the writings of Sayyid Quṭb who infused aspects of his socialist, communist past into his interpretation of early Islāmic history. After judging every Muslim society on Earth of reverting to pre-Islāmic barbarism (*jāhiliyyah*) and apostasy (*riddah*), he openly called for destructive, violent revolutions to overthrow all of those societies.[202] **Taqī al-Dīn al-Nabhānī**, a former Baʿthist, Communist Nationalist, erected his political group, Ḥizb al-Taḥrīr, upon a similar track, having himself participated in intrigues and revolutionary plots. He portrayed Islām as a revolutionary ideology aimed at toppling tyrants. Likewise, the writings of **Abū Aʿlā**

Shīʿite thought. Sayyid Quṭb excommunicated many of the Prophet's Companions through his extremist anti-Islāmic ideology and spread hatred against Muslim societies. Refer to the section which follows on Sayyid Quṭb.

200 "O" News Agency, 14th October, 2013, http://onaeg.com/?p=1219303.

201 The famous example was the assassination of the Egyptian Prime Minister, Maḥmūd al-Naqrāshī on 28th December 1948. Days later, the Salafī scholar, Shaykh Aḥmad Shākir, issued a statement condemning the assassination, declaring those who perpetrate political assassinations to be apostates from Islām and not merely sinful Muslims. He declared them to be the Khārijites whom the Prophet (ﷺ) warned against. This statement was published in the magazine al-Asās on 2nd January 1949 in an article titled *al-Īmān Qayd al-Fatk*.

202 These writings are very apparent in his Qur'ān commentary known as "*Fī Ẓilāl al-Qur'ān*" (In the Shade of the Qur'ān) extracts of which were published separately as "*Maʿālim Fī al-Tarīq*" (Milestones).

Mawdūdī who portrayed the message of the Prophets as being one of violent revolutions. The writings of these men paved the way for the ideology of mass takfīr (excommunication) to appear and spread in the minds of Muslims and prepared the ground for a twisted notion of jihād. This 20th century notion of jihād became the springboard for groups like al-Takfīr wal-Hijrah, al-Qā'idah and ISIS.[203] As for the claim that the ideological basis for extremism and terrorism is found in the works of Ibn Taymiyyah and Muḥammad bin 'Abd al-Wahhāb, this is a lie repeated in academia and media. The truth is that when the Muslims in the Gulf countries abandoned the books of the Salafī scholars and turned to the books of ideology (*fikr*) - such as those of Sayyid Quṭb, his brother Moḥammad Quṭb, Abū A'lā Mawdūdī, Taqī al-Dīn al-Nabhānī and others - the doctrines of mass excommunication (*takfīr*) and hatred of Muslim societies appeared. Then terrorism perpetrated in the name of jihād began to plague Muslim countries before it showed up in the West.

The late Salafī scholar, **Shaykh Ibn al-'Uthaymīn** (رَحِمَهُ ٱللَّهُ) said, "When the affair of al-Ikhwān (the Muslim Brotherhood) appeared, the ones who proceed without wisdom, the westeners' perception of Islām became increasingly disfigured. I am referring to those who throw bombs into crowds of people with the claim that this is jihād in the path of Allāh! The reality is that they have harmed Islām and the people of Islām. A person has to almost cover his face so that he is not associated with this seditious terrorizing faction. Islām is free and innocent of them."[204] Credible academics, researchers and authors have correctly pointed out that the methodology of Sayyid Quṭb is taken directly from Marxism and Leninism, is distinctly European in its origin and has simply been veiled with Islāmic terminology.

---

[203] To learn more about the realities of these heads of misguidance refer to **ikhwanis.com**, **sayyidqutb.com** and **nabahani.com**.

[204] Refer to *Fatāwā 'Ulamā al-Kibār* (p. 321-322). These types of actions were perpetrated by followers of Ḥasan al-Bannā in the late 1940s and were advocated against society by Sayyid Quṭb in his prison writings during the 1960s prior to his execution.

Sayyid Quṭb: Grandfather of Contemporary Takfīrī Jihādī Groups

Sayyid Quṭb was born in to a Ṣūfī family in 1906 in the Asyūt district of Egypt and was nurtured upon the tradition of attachment and devotion to saints.[205] As a youth he indulged in astrology and magic and would be solicited by young women to perform spells mostly for relationships. After graduating in Cairo in 1924 he worked as a teacher and editor and entered into the phase of materialist philosophies, doubt and atheism.[206] During the 1930s Quṭb would write in numerous newspaper columns and on one occasion he made a call for open nudity in the streets of Cairo. He defended this view in a piece in al-Ahrām on 10th July 1938. He was refuted, sarcastically, by Muḥammad Husayn Abū Sālim in another newspaper, al-Nadhīr on 18th July 1938. In 1939 he published a research piece which was later published as *al-Taṣwīr al-Fannī Fil Qur'ān* (The Depiction of Art in the Qur'ān). Within this work he mocked and reviled numerous lofty Prophets of Allāh, from them Abraham, Moses, Solomon, David (عَلَيْهِمُالسَّلَامُ) and he also made insinuations against the Prophet Jesus (عَلَيْهِالسَّلَامُ) and his mother Mary (عَلَيْهَاالسَّلَامُ). Quṭb's writings on Islām were from a purely literary perspective during the 1940s and not connected to Islamic doctrine. He was a literary artist, a writer and also dabbled unsuccessfully in poetry. In some of his poems he would write in graphic detail in

[205] The intent in this tradition of venerating saints is to solicit aid, rescue and intercession from them and is an imitation of the Christians in their saint-worship. The Sharī'ah has outlined the true status of the Prophets and the Righteous and given Muslims the moderate, balanced path regarding how to respect them without falling into exaggeration and opposing the Sharī'ah. The exaggeration in the status of the righteous fosters a mystical and mythical cult-like following of pious saints whose veneration is alleged to bring easy salvation. For many people, this relieves the burden of authentic religious observance and allows a nominal, superficial attachment to Islām.

[206] Ṣalāh al-Khālidi, in his detailed biographical account of Sayyid Quṭb titled *Sayyid Quṭb Min al-Mīlād ilā al-Istish-hād* states that Quṭb entered a phase of doubt and atheism for around 15 years of his life in which he engrossed himself in European materialist philosophies.

matters of love and sensuality. Helmy Namnam, an Egyptian journalist who authored a book on the 1952 Socialist revolution in which Quṭb is said to have played a role, writes in this book that Quṭb used to visit bars every now and then for a sip of cognac.[207]

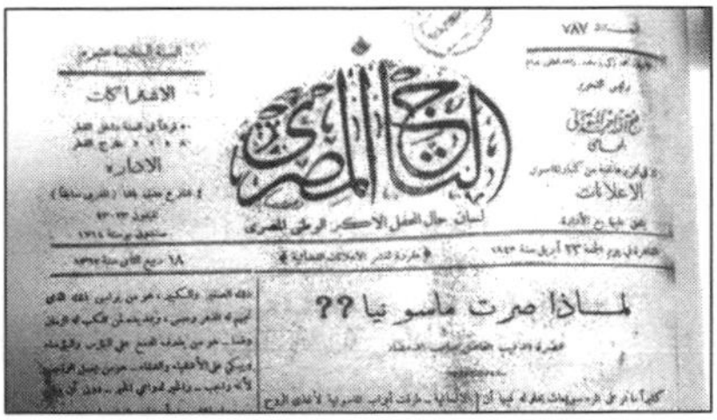
التاج المصري
الاشتراكات
الادارة
الإعلانات
لماذا صرت ماسونيا ؟؟

Research has revealed that Sayyid Quṭb used to write for the official mouthpiece of the Grand Freemasonic Lodge known as *al-Tāj al-Miṣrī* (*The Egyptian Crown*) during the Second World War in the early 1940s.[208] Quṭb had the privilege of writing the main editorial. On the cover page of each edition there occurs, "Edited by Senior Freemasons." In the 23rd April 1943 edition of *al-Tāj al-Miṣrī,* Quṭb's opening editorial piece was titled "*Why Did I Become a Freemason?*" In another article published in the edition of 14th May 1943, Quṭb wrote a piece titled, "*Musānadah al-Ḥulafāʾ wal-Tahakkum ʿalā Khuṣumihim*" (Supporting the Allies and Taunting Their Opponents) - referring to the Allied Forces of US and Britain against Germany. He wrote, "Indeed truth has come, and falsehood has vanished. Rather, the truth has been aided and the treacherous have perished. The signs of victory are flapping with glow and pride. The desert has emptied save from its righteous, loyal men. For the men of truth and the messengers of democracy were able to repel the plot of the plotters and throw it back upon them." These writings in this Freemasonic newspaper carried a strong religious spirit within them as is clear from the language used. In these same writings, Quṭb described the English and Americans as "*mujāḥidīn*" (wagers of jihād), "*rusul al-dīmuqrāṭiyah*" (messengers of democracy), "*rijāl al-ḥaqq*" (men of truth), "*ḥulafāʾunā*" (our allies), "*ikhwānunā*" (our brothers), and he made supplication for them

[207] In *Sayyid Quṭb wa Thawrah Yūlyu* (Cairo, 1999, p.40).

[208] From the writers and researchers who have pointed this out include Tharwat al-Khirbāwī in his book *Sirr al-Maʿbad* and Wāʾīl Dusūqī in his Master's thesis on Freemasonry in Egypt from 1798 to 1964.

"*Allāhu ma'akum*" (Allāh is with you). He also used Qur'ānic terminology through which he declared the ideology of freedom and democracy which the Allied Forces were fighting for as "*truth in the face of which falsehood has perished*," an expression taken from the Qur'ān. One would hardly think that this man, his writings and his ideology are behind the ideology and activities of al-Qā'idah and ISIS.

In 1948 Quṭb went to the United States and remained there for two years. During that period he travelled extensively, meeting with figures of different backgrounds. He mentioned how he was a member of various non-Islāmic religious associations and participated in their events. On his return to Egypt he wrote of his stay in Greeley in Colorado as an example of what he experienced. [209] When he came back, Quṭb took a new direction. In 1951, he wrote the book *Ma'rakat al-Islām wal-Ra'samāliyyah* (The Battle Between Islām and Capitalism) and a little later in the same year, *al-Salām al-'Ālamī wal-Islām* (World Peace and Islām). In this latter book, he speaks of the Muslims needing a Communist type military that would scare the tyrants. He also began writing articles in numerous newsletters such as *al-Da'wah* which belonged to al-Ikhwān and also *al-Liwā' al-Jadīd*. It was the same year in which he started writing his commentary of the Qur'ān, *Fī Ẓilāl al-Qur'ān* (In the Shade of the Qur'ān). In all of these writings it was clear that he was pushing a new orientation under the flag of Islām. In his book *al-'Adālah al-Ijtimā'iyyah Fī al-Islām* (Social Justice in Islām) and *Kutub wa Shakhṣiyāt* (Books and Personalities), Quṭb interpreted early Islāmic history through a Marxist, Socialist, Communist lens, reviled

[209] Quṭb wrote about this in an article titled *Laylah Ḥamrā'* (A Red Night) which he wrote in al-Risālah newsletter in 1951 after his return. In this article he speaks of his attendance of an event in a church in Greely, Colorado. He states "I was a member of its association just as I was a member of the associations of numerous religious bodies in the various places in which I lived." Qutb recounts this also in his book *al-Islām wa Mushkilāt al-Ḥaḍārah* (p. 86). However, this was not a one off event. Quṭb mentions that he travelled all across the United States and took up membership with different associations and clubs. He also met with figures in politics and academic institutions.

the third Caliph ʿUthmān (رَضِيَٱللَّٰهُعَنْهُ) and excommunicated Muʿāwiyah (رَضِيَٱللَّٰهُعَنْهُ) and the rulers of Banū Umayyah, accusing them of mismanagement, hoarding capital and creating class separation. He praised the revolution initiated and led by ʿAbdullāh bin Sabaʾ[210] which led to the assassination of ʿUthmān (رَضِيَٱللَّٰهُعَنْهُ) and described it as a manifestation of the "true Islāmic spirit."

In these writings is an ideological framework identical to the ideology of the Khārijites and of socialist, communist movements who operate under the banner of social justice and equal distribution of wealth. Thus, in this period Quṭb started writing about Islām from a doctrinal angle, unlike his previous phrase, in which his interest was purely artistic and literary.[211] This ideological framework is greatly reminiscent of the slogan of "social justice" raised by Dhul-Khuwayṣarah al-Tamīmī, the father of the Khārijites who accused the Prophet Muḥammad (صَلَّى ٱللَّٰهُ عَلَيْهِ وَسَلَّمَ) of being unjust in the distribution of

---

[210] The 1906 edition of the Jewish Encyclopedia has an entry for Abdullāh bin Sabaʾ as follows, "A Jew of Yemen, Arabia, of the seventh century, who settled in Medina and embraced Islam. Having adversely criticized Calif Othman's administration, he was banished from the town. Thence he went to Egypt, where he founded an antiothmanian sect, to promote the interests of Ali. On account of his learning he obtained great influence there, and formulated the doctrine that, just as every prophet had an assistant who afterward succeeded him, Mohammed's vizier was Ali, who had therefore been kept out of the califate by deceit. Othman had no legal claim whatever to the califate; and the general dissatisfaction with his government greatly contributed to the spread of Abdallah's teachings. Tradition relates that when Ali had assumed power, Abdallah ascribed divine honors to him by addressing him with the words, 'Thou art Thou!' Thereupon Ali banished him to Madain. After Ali's assassination Abdallah is said to have taught that Ali was not dead but alive, and had never been killed; that a part of the Deity was hidden in him; and that after a certain time he would return to fill the earth with justice. Till then the divine character of Ali was to remain hidden in the imams, who temporarily filled his place. It is easy to see that the whole idea rests on that of the Messiah in combination with the legend of Elijah the prophet." End of quote. This entry indicates the origins of the Shiʿite sect.

[211] Quṭb's early writings were simply artistic and literary discussions of the style of the Qurʾān and were not studies on Islāmic subjects.

wealth and from whose descendants, the Prophet informed, would come the Khārijites who would depart from Islām and, motivated by other than Islām, would fight and kill the Muslims. In 1952, Quṭb was said to be involved in the socialist coup of Jamāl Abd al-Nāsir. For some reason, he fell out with the Free Officers in 1953 and was given a prominent position by the then supreme guide and leader of the Muslim Brotherhood, Ḥasan al-Ḥudaybī, who was also a fellow freemason.[212] It was in this decade, within Nāsserite Egypt, that Quṭb's extremist doctrines began to take shape. In this period, his hatred of all Islāmic societies, his excommunication of them (judging them with apostasy) and instigating violent jihāds against them began to take shape in his writings. He explicitly negated the Islām of all contemporary societies and conveyed the idea that there has been no Islāmic society in existence since the time of Banū Umayyah.

Thus, after Quṭb announced his hatred and excommunication of all Muslim societies, governments and institutions without exception, in a hateful, thunderous tone, he advocated violent revolutions against them. These particular writings of Quṭb were strongly influenced by Marxist, Communist revolutionary movements. His famous tract known as Milestones[213] is modelled around Lenin's work "*What is to be done?*" In addition to the notion of social justice, Quṭb's ideology took shape around a number of other concepts such as *Jāhiliyyah*[214] and *Ḥākimiyyah*. The first alludes to all contemporary Muslim societies reverting to the pre-Islamic days of ignorance through which they are judged apostates. The second alludes to the sole right of Allāh alone to judge which Quṭb alleged to have been usurped by all rulers and governments. Within this framework, Sayyid Quṭb redefined the

---

[212] It is almighty strange that the alleged Muslim Brotherhood had, at the very peak of its leadership, heads in Freemasonry.

[213] This is the manifesto of every modern-day Takfīrī and Jihādī and all acts of terrorism have their ideological foundation in the writings of Sayyid Quṭb.

[214] In this concept Sayyid Quṭb was influenced by the French Philosopher, Alexis Carrell and his book, "Man, the Unknown" in which the idea of "barbarism" of modern societies is developed.

notion of jihād and took it away from its noble and honorable status to one involving terrorism, chaos, treachery, perfidy, slaughtering of civilians and everything that opposes the spirit of Islām. Thus, all contemporary takfīrī and jihādī movements are operating upon the philosophy and thought (*fikr*) of Sayyid Quṭb and not the Islām of Muḥammad (ﷺ) and his Companions which is based upon revelation (*waḥī*). Sayyid Quṭb expressed numerous statements of apostasy which are present in his writings, the most apparent of which is his mockery of the Prophets. From the contemporary Salafī scholars are those who either express or accommodate the view that Quṭb was an apostate, a disbeliever and not a Muslim.[215]

The followers of his ideology are known as Quṭbiyyah and over the past 30 years, they have been instrumental in spreading the Khārijite ideology amongst Muslims. Some of the key figures of this orientation who are directly responsible for promulgating the doctrines of the Khārijites include, Salmān al-Awdah, Safar al-Ḥawālī, Nāṣir al-ʿUmar, ʿĀʾiḍ al-Qarnī, ʿAbd al-Raḥmān ʿAbd al-Khāliq, ʿAdnān ʿArʿūr, Abū Muḥammad al-Maqdisī, Abū Qatādah al-Filistīnī, Sulaymān al-ʿUlwān, Usāmah bin Lādin, Ayman al-Zawāhirī, other figures of al-Qāʿidah[216] and more recently ISIS and al-Nuṣrah. In the West, those responsible for the spread of this ideology include **Ali al-Timīmī** who was a leading Quṭbī spokesman doing the rounds between Britain and the US in the 1990s and early 2000s. He is currently serving a life-sentence in the United States on terrorism related charges. Al-Timīmī was outspoken

---

[215] It is related that Shaykh Ismāʿīl al-Anṣārī, the scholar of al-Madīnah, would make excommunicate Sayyid Quṭb. The late Salafī scholar, Shaykh Ibn al-ʿUthaymīn said, "Had he been alive, we would have declared him a disbeliever." And Shaykh ʿUbayd al-Jābirī, another scholar of al-Madīnah, said, "I do not find fault with anyone who declares Sayyid Quṭb a disbeliever in my presence."

[216] In the 1990s these individuals played an instrumental role in spreading the extremist ideology which today fuels and propels the ISIS machine of terror. Yet every last one of these treacherous criminals is now trying to wash his hands clean of ISIS after observing the inevitable consequence of the deviant, extremist ideas they were pushing two decades ago.

in his fallacious claim that the Salafī way had been hijacked by a small group[217] as part of a worldwide conspiracy to revise Islām and alter its concepts in order to "support the new world order." That Sayyid Quṭb has been exposed as a Freemason will forever haunt al-Timīmī whose wild conspiracy theory has been rendered quackery by brute fact and harsh reality. On the contrary, the religion of Islām was hijacked by dubious, shady figures such as Sayyid Quṭb whose harm upon Islām and the Muslims has known no equal in the 20th and 21st centuries.[218] It is the evil 20th century takfīrī jihādī ideology which is more worthy of being considered an effective conspirational tool for instigating turmoil in Muslim lands or countries, destabilizing them, hijacking their politics and economies and generally hampering their progress which would have been for the benefit of their own subjects.

Many takfīrī, jihādī khārijite groups conceal themselves under the veil of Salafiyyah despite having little, if anything, to do with it.[219] It is

---

[217] Those targeted by this conspiracy theory were the Salafī scholars who played an instrumental role in bringing awareness to the Muslims at large of the evils of the Muslim Brotherhood (al-Ikhwān) and the evil, destructive doctrines of Ḥasan al-Banna and Sayyid Quṭb and of whoever played a role in spreading them within unsuspecting Salafī circles.

[218] The Prophetic traditions clash with European materialist philosophies in that Muslims are ordered to have patience upon the tyranny and oppression of the rulers and upon economic and social injustice in order to preserve general stabiity and security. Further, these calamities are due to the sins and transgressions of the servants themselves and thus the true means of rectification do not lie fundamentally in removing rulers and toppling governments. The modern-day takfīrī jihādī Khārijites therefore are simply a by-product of 19th and 20th century European revolutionary philosophies which had an influence upon individuals like Abū Aʿlā Mawdūdī, Sayyid Quṭb and Taqī al-Dīn al-Nabhānī. All of them preached violent revolutions (preceded by ideological revolutions) as a means of restoring the Khilāfah, as they claim, and in this methodology they have followed neither the Prophet of Islām (ﷺ) nor his Companions nor the Righteous Predecessors.

[219] Groups such as Ḥizb al-Taḥrīr and figures such as Omar Bakrī and Anjem Choudary and their followers conceal themselves under the veil of Salafiyyah. This is done on purely tactical grounds because the Salafīs are the ones who exposed them and their deviant doctrines during the 1990s. They

here that non-Muslims, their politicians, governments and academics are advised to be aware of the incorrect fallacious grouping of Salafīs into three factions: The Salafi reformists, the Salafi jihadists[220] and the Salafi activists.[221] The latter two groups are not Salafīs, they are Khārijites. They only differ with each other in the extent to which takfīr (excommunication) or killing feature in their activities. But the basic idea, that Islāmic reform must come by toppling rulers or taking power through whatever means are available, *including participation in democracy*, is the core of Khārijite philosophy. In reality, it is just a means to acquire power and wealth. The philosophy provides the excuse and is clothed with lofty Islāmic slogans to make it appealing. They are the ones spoken about very harshly by the Prophet (ﷺ) in many authentic traditions as has preceded. Their mention, refutation and condemnation is consistent throughout fourteen centuries of Salafī scholarship starting from the Companion ʿAlī bin Abī Ṭālib (رضي الله عنه), the erudite scholar amongst the Companions, Ibn ʿAbbās (رضي الله عنهما), then through the centuries and ages right until this day of ours with scholars such as Shaykh al-Albānī, Shaykh Ibn Bāz, Shaykh Ibn al-ʿUthaymīn, Shaykh al-Fawzān, Shaykh Rabī bin Hādī, Shaykh Zayd al-Madkhalī, Shaykh ʿAbdullāh al-Ghudayān, Shaykh ʿAbd al-Muḥsin al-ʿAbbād, Shaykh ʿUbayd al-Jābirī, Shaykh Muḥammad bin Hādī and many others.

Once the above is clear, it is important that imposters speaking in the name of Islām in the Western lands are identified and recognized.

---

found that identifying with Salafiyyah whilst concealing the foundations of their heresy would be a way to penetrate Muslim circles and push their evil ideology. In turn, Salafīs would be labelled as the extremists and terrorists - and so they achieve two objectives. First, to spread their extremism and second to make the focus and scrutiny more widely distributed so it falls not upon them specifically, but upon Salafīs as a whole.

[220] Such as al-Qāʿidah, ISIS and others who engage in terrorism.

[221] They are said to be the political Salafīs who engage in activism or participate in democracy and elections. Their objectives are essentially the same as the Jihādī Takfīris - pursuit of power.

Imposters Speaking in the Name of Islām

In Britain, numerous European lands, many of the central Asian states and less so in Canada and the US there are to be found imposters speaking in the name of Islām and Sunnah.[222] The ideological origin of these imposters lies with **Ḥizb al-Taḥrīr**, founded by **Taqī al-Dīn al-Nabhānī**. However, due to the way this group was exposed and refuted by Salafī Muslims in the UK in particular throughout the 1990s and early 2000s, they started altering their labels and outer garments. They have previously assumed names such as *al-Muhājirūn* (the Emigrants), *al-Firqah al-Nājiyah* (the Saved Sect), *Ahl al-Sunnah wal-Jamāʿah* (the People of Prophetic Tradition and Unity), *al-Ghurabā* (the Strangers) and *Islām4uk*. In recent years they have settled on the label of Salafiyyah. This is a deliberate strategy on their behalf and has two main objectives. Firstly, to conceal the true and real underlying ideology they are promoting, an approach which constitutes coating their poison with honey. Secondly, to deflect criticism and prevent exposure in the sense that their ideology, their extremism and sympathy towards terrorists and extremists can be ascribed more broadly to the Salafī way and its genuine adherents to which they are the staunchest of enemies. There are counterparts to these people in France, Belgium, Germany, Netherlands and other places.[223] As we have already established, 20th century Khārijite takfīrī jihādism has its origins in the distillation of European philosophies in the mind of Sayyid Quṭb and his writings from the late 1940s onwards. There is a similar pattern with other movements which appeared at the same time. Taqī al-Dīn al-Nabhānī, the founder of Ḥizb al-Taḥrīr has doctrinal roots that lie in the Ṣūfī Ashʿarī tradition along with Muʿtazilī influences. In the late 1940s he was involved in Baʿthist Communist and Nationalist movements. He was sent by ʿAbdullah al-

[222] And some of them, in the name of Salafiyyah as will be discussed.

[223] Amongst the covert Taḥrīrīs are those who do not make open ascription to Salafiyyah such as Anjem Choudary. Others who became affected by the call of the Quṭbiyyah such as Safar al-Ḥawālī and his likes donned the gown of Salafiyyah as a means of camouflaging their caliphate-centric ideology.

Tall to Husnī Zaʿīm in Damascus in 1949 to help engineer a revolution in Jordan after a successful coup had taken place in Syria in April of the same year, indicating that he was already involved in clandestine, revolutionary activities. Al-Nabhānī set up the organization of Ḥizb al-Taḥrīr in 1953, modelling it on the secretive Baʿthist parties which he was involved in during the late 1940s. It is a fact that the structure of Hizb al-Taḥrīr as an organization is based directly on the Communist "cell." They would operate as a tight, rigid party with indoctrination upon the works of al-Nabhānī being fundamental to engineering revolution. In fact, their entire approach is identical to Communist revolutionism. Al-Nabhānī simply "islamicized" the Communist mode of operandum in the same way that Sayyid Quṭb clothed Leninism in Islāmic Garb. The 20th century Khilāfah movements are inspired by these types of materialist revolutionary ideologies which are alien to Islām. The explanations and causes behind the rise and decline, honouring and humiliation of nations outlined in the Qurʾān and Prophetic traditions fundamentally clash with this approach which is distinctly European.[224]

Once this is understood, imposters such as Anjem Choudary can be seen for what they are. The real underlying ideology being preached by them is **Communist revolution** glorified with Islāmic terminology

[224] That which is in the Prophetic traditions is, for example, that when the Muslims cheat in weights in measures, it is the rule of Allāh that they will be inflicted with famine, hardship, scarcity and **the tyranny of the ruler**. And when they withhold the zakāh (obligatory charity), droughts will descend upon them. And when they break their covenant of worshipping Allāh alone, their enemies will be given power over them and they will take out of their hands what they possess, as occurs in the authentic Prophetic tradition of ʿAbdullah bin ʿUmar (رَضِيَٱللَّهُعَنْهُ) related by Ibn Mājah (no. 4019). Likewise, when they engage in forbidden transactions, become content with agriculture and pursue the world, humiliation will descend upon them as occurs in the tradition also related by ʿAbdullāh bin ʿUmar (رَضِيَٱللَّهُعَنْهُ) and collected by Abū Dāwūd and others. In light of these and many other texts, it is clear that the methodologies of these 20th century Khārijite, takfirī jihādists are founded upon compound ignorance and not knowledge. They do not appreciate the laws of Allāh in His creation and mistake effects for their causes.

such as "*Establishing the Sharīʿah*" and "*Establishing the Khilāfah.*" Ignorant and sentimental Muslims are taken in by the beautified rhetoric and think that protests, demonstrations, agitations and revolutions are the solution for every problem whose responsibility is placed squarely upon rulers alone.

Dr. Aḥmad al-Mawṣilī writes in *Encyclopedia of Islamic Movements in the Arabic Nation, Turkey and Iran*, under an-Nabhani's entry (p. 407), "For a period of time, he adopted the doctrine of the Baʿthist Party." In the book, *Shaykh Taqī al-Dīn al-Nabahānī, the Caller of the Islamic Caliphate*, (2009), Hishām ʿUlaywān writes, "And in addition to the structural (organizational) resemblance between Ḥizb al-Taḥrīr and the (Arab) nationalistic parties, it is possible to note the aspects of resemblance in content and terminology between the discourse of Michel Aflaq, the founder of Baʿthism himself, and the discourse of al-Nabahani, especially (in the period) before his founding of Ḥizb al-Taḥrīr..." Al-Nabhānī took what he learned through his experience with the Arabic Baʿthist Nationalist movements and developed his liberationist ideology out of it. Like Communist, Marxist, Leninist movements, the idea is to topple the ruling authorities and impose a system from the top. This is not Islām and Islām was not established like this. The Prophets and Messengers invited people to Islām by explaining its greatest foundation, Tawḥīd. It's simplicity, beauty, fruits and life-changing effects captured their hearts. But al-Nabhānī distorted the Prophetic biography in order to make it fit with the Communist revolutionary protocol outlined in his writings and claimed the Prophet (ﷺ) called to an ideological, then practical revolution and then imposed his "system." This distortion of the Prophetic biography underlies all the rhetoric coming from charlatans such as Anjem Choudary and his followers who are upon the methodology of Ḥizb al-Taḥrīr whilst faking attachment to Salafiyyah. It is sad that imposters like them are given air time on mass media to perpetuate the distortion of the principle message of Islām in front of tens of millions of non-Muslims. This also demonstrates that the mass-media is complicit in generating fear and hatred towards Muslims.

European Materialist Philosophy and 20th Century Khārijite Movements

In this section we will establish through citations from Western academics that extremist ideologies are alien to Islām. The ideological foundations of 20th and 21st century terrorism attributed to Islām *and* the ideological basis upon which mockery is made of the Prophet Muḥammad (ﷺ) have something in common. Their roots lie in materialist, atheistic philosophies of Europe and are fundamentally European in nature.

In a 2003 article, Daniel Brogan wrote "Quṭb's work is to militant Islām what Das Kapital was to Communism."[225] Ladan and Roya Boroumand wrote, "Like Mawdudi and various Western totalitarians, he [Quṭb] identified his own society (in his case, contemporary Muslim polities) as among the enemies that a virtuous, ideologically self-conscious, vanguard minority would have to fight by any means necessary, including violent revolution, so that a new and perfectly just society might arise. His ideal society was a classless one where the 'selfish individual' of liberal democracies would be banished and the 'exploitation of man by man' would be abolished. God alone would govern it through the implementation of Islamic law (shariʿa). This was Leninism in Islāmist dress."[226] Paul Berman wrote in an article published in the New York Times, 23rd March 2003, "The few had to gather themselves together into what Quṭb in 'Milestones' called a vanguard - a term that he must have borrowed from Lenin." Rod Dreher wrote, "What is to be done? Lenin famously asked about Czarist Russia. Quṭb's answer to the same question about the West was, in part, 'Milestones,' a Leninist-style tract advocating worldwide Islāmic revolution."[227] Phil Paine writes, "The first thing one notices

---

[225] *Al Qaeda's Greeley Roots*, June 2003.

[226] In an article titled *Terror, Islam and Democracy*, Journal of Democracy 13.2 (2002) 5-20.

[227] In the Dallas Morning News (27th August 2006).

about Quṭb's ideological thought is how little it has to do with traditions of Islām, or the needs of people in Islāmic countries. It is profoundly European in inspiration, and it's chief models are Hitler, Marx and Lenin... Lenin is by far the strongest influence. Whole passages look like they were simply copied out from his works and then a pseudo-Islāmic terminology inserted, 'revolutionary vanguard' becoming 'Islamic vanguard', and so on... As Marxist mumbo-jumbo justified the telling of any lie, the betrayal of any value, the commitment of any atrocity, in the name of an implacable destiny, so too, does Milestones."[228] Lawrence Wright observed about the book 'Milestones,' that "Its ringing apocalyptic tone may be compared with Rousseau's 'Social Contract' and Lenin's 'What Is to Be Done?' - with similar bloody consequences."[229]

John Gray writes, "Islamic fundamentalism is not an indigenous growth. It is an exotic hybrid, bred from the encounter of sections of the Islamic intelligentsia with radical western ideologies. In *A Fury for God*, Malise Ruthven shows that Sayyid Quṭb, an Egyptian executed after imprisonment in 1966 and arguably the most influential ideologue of radical Islam, incorporated many elements derived from European ideology into his thinking. For example, the idea of a revolutionary vanguard of militant believers does not have an Islamic pedigree. It is 'a concept imported from Europe, through a lineage that stretches back to the Jacobins, through the Bolsheviks and latter-day Marxist guerrillas such as the Baader-Meinhof gang.' In a brilliantly illuminating and arrestingly readable analysis, Ruthven demonstrates the close affinities between radical Islamist thought and the vanguard of modernist and postmodern thinking in the West. The inspiration for Quṭb's thought is not so much the Koran, but the current of western philosophy embodied in thinkers such as Nietzsche, Kierkegaard and Heidegger. Quṭb's thought - the blueprint for all subsequent radical Islamist political theology - is as much a

[228] In his review article, *The Ideology of Sayyid Quṭb* (22nd August 2006)

[229] Cited by Daniel Martin in *Sayyid Quṭb: The Father of Al-Qaida*, published in the Independent in August 2006.

response to 20th-century Europe's experience of 'the death of God' as to anything in the Islamic tradition. Quṭbism is in no way traditional. Like all fundamentalist ideology, it is unmistakeably modern."[230]

The ideological roots of terrorism have no basis in Islām. It's basis lies in discontentment in matters of wealth and the desire for power and authority - it is purely a material thing. Indeed, this was the very first slogan raised by the ideological grandfather of the Khārijite terrorists, as has preceded. The man known as **Dhul-Khuwaiṣarah al-Tamimī** challenged the Prophet (ﷺ) and questioned his integrity in the matter of distribution of wealth and said, "We are more worthy of this (wealth) than them," meaning the tribes to whom wealth was distributed for reasons of benefit which the Prophet had in mind. About him, the Prophet said, "*From this man's offspring will appear a people who recite the Qur'an but it will not go beyond their throats.*" He further described these people, "*They are the most evil of the creation*" and he stated, "*Each time they appear, they will be cut off until the Dajjāl (Anti-Christ) will appear in the midst of their armies*" and "*If I was to reach them, I would slaughter them, like the slaughtering of ʿĀd (a destroyed nation of the past)*" meaning, every last one of them until none of them remain. It is not surprising then, that the roots of modern terrorism lie in the writings of a man, Sayyid Quṭb, whose background lies in Communist, Socialist, material philosophies and who brought that poison into his writings on Islām, thereby reviving the ideology of the Khārijite terrorists of takfīr (excommunication) and revolution.[231]

---

[230] In his article, *How Marx Turned Muslim*, in the Independent, 27th July 2002.

[231] Shaykh Rabīʿ bin Hādī, a Salafī scholar from Saudi Arabia who has played the single most instrumental role in exposing and refuting Sayyid Quṭb, his evil ideology and his fabrications against Islām and Muslim societies through numerous works and publications, wrote, "I consider, by Allāh, his ideology... is a plot against Islām, his history is dark, a Communist history, bewildered, a secularist with the Wafd party, with Tāhā Ḥusayn, with al-ʿAqqād, and he would read Western philosophy to the end of it. He went to the West, to America and remained there for two years and learned Freemasonry." Refer to Shaykh Rabīʿ's two volume Fatāwā collection (1/525-526). Evidence firmly

The ideological roots of this evil trace back to the same place (Europe) from where that Existentialist, nihilist philosophy is propounded on the basis of which the Prophet of Islām (صَلَّىٰ ٱللَّهُ عَلَيْهِ وَسَلَّمَ) is lied upon, mocked and ridiculed for something he is free and innocent of. And it is justified in the name of the *freedom of speech* and the *right to offend* - even if it involves blatant lies.

Rather than depicting the Prophet Muḥammad (صَلَّىٰ ٱللَّهُ عَلَيْهِ وَسَلَّمَ) through satirical cartoons having no basis in fact, it is closer to truth and justice that the likes of Marx and Lenin or the heads of European states are depicted crying and remorseful for the destruction that European materialist philosophies and their *methodologies* have inflicted upon Islām, its lands and its people[232] through the hands of misguided wandering strayers such as Sayyid Quṭb who infused such poison into a corrupt reading of Islām and its texts. This gave birth to takfīrī revolutionary movements and ideologies of hatred towards Muslim societies against whom terrorism and violence is justified with gross distortions of texts from the Qur'ān and Prophetic traditions *before* it is justified against non-Muslims.

The likes of al-Qā'idah and ISIS do not represent Islām, they represent their own interests. Their terrorist activity in the West is not the foundation but the branch. In its foundations, their hatred and terror is directed towards Muslim societies and it has never been otherwise since they first appeared 1400 years ago. The only difference in the 20th and 21st centuries is that they resent the meddling of the West in Muslim lands because it greatly hinders the progression of their own agenda in those same lands. Exponentially more Muslims have been killed as a direct result of this foreign, poisonous, alien-to-Islām ideology in the past 30-40 years than have non-Muslims in the same period.

---

indicates that Sayyid Quṭb was involved in Freemasonry way earlier, from the late 1930s or before.

[232] In addition to the tens of millions of Chinese, Russians and others who suffered under Communism.

Closing Notes

The Prophet Muḥammad (ﷺ) is too noble and dignified than that his status as the humble Messenger of Allāh and the most honourable and influential man on Earth should be affected by resentful, spite-filled existentialist nihilists and those with hearts similiar to them. It is upon all Muslims in all places to behave and act with dignity and honour and not to behave like animals, rioting on the streets. Not the least amount of harm reaches the Prophet of Islām (ﷺ) because Allāh has sufficed him against the mockers. Allāh (عَزَّوَجَلَّ) said, "**And already were messengers ridiculed before you, but those who mocked them were enveloped by what they used to ridicule.**" (21:41) and He said, "**Indeed, We are sufficient for you against the mockers.**" (15:95). The way to counter this rhetoric is by clarifying the truth, removing the misconceptions and educating people about this noble Prophet of Islām (ﷺ), the loftiness of his message and the loftiness of his character. Terrorism benefits no one and its greatest harm is upon Islām and the Muslims themselves. So just as we defend and exonerate the honour of Muḥammad (ﷺ) from the spiteful existentialists, we also defend and exonerate Islām and what was brought by the Prophet (ﷺ) from the ideology and activity of the most evil of creation, the worst of those killed under the sky, *the Khārijite Dogs of Hellfire* as the Prophet (ﷺ) aptly described them in what is firmly established from him. For it is their evil ideology and its consequences which inspired the spiteful atheists and nihilists to make mockery of the Prophet of Islām (ﷺ) with lies and fabrications in the first place.

In closing, all praise is due Allāh and may the peace and blessings be upon the last and final Prophet, Muḥammad, and all the Prophets of God - including those sent to the Children of Isra'īl such as Moses, Solomon, David, Jesus and John - for all the Prophets of God are brethren, their way is one and it is Islām.

Further Reading

SCHOLARLY WORKS, TREATISES AND RESOURCES ON TERRORISM

◈ **Terrorism and its Effects Upon the Individual and Society** by Shaykh Zayd al-Madkhalī.

◈ **With Which Intellect and Religiosity is Bombing and Destruction Considered Jihād?** by Shaykh ʿAbd al-Muḥsin al-Abbād.

◈ **The Rise of Jihādist Extremism in the West** by Salafī Publications.

The following websites provide useful information about extremist ideologies and their proponents: **takfiris.com**, **sayyidqutb.com**, **nabahani.com**, **islamagainstextremism.com** and **shariah.ws.**

Visit: **www.prophetmuhammad.name** to learn more about the biography of the Prophet (ﷺ) and the teachings of Islām.

RESEARCH ON ISLAMOPHOBIC HATE NETWORKS

A number of in depth academic research papers expose the funders of hate who help shape public opinion against Muslims.

◈ **The Cold War on British Muslims.**
An examination of Policy Exchange and the Centre for Social Cohesion. Refer to www.spinwatch.org.

◈ **Fear Inc. The Roots of the Islamophobia Network in America.**
This in-depth investigation conducted by the Center for American Progress Action Fund reveals not a vast right-wing conspiracy behind the rise of Islamophobia in our nation but rather a small, tightly networked group of misinformation experts guiding an effort that reaches millions of Americans through effective advocates, media partners, and grassroots organizing. This spreading of hate and misinformation primarily starts with five key people and their organizations, which are sustained by funding from a clutch of key foundations. Refer to www.americanprogress.org.